ABBREVIATE
uh BREE vee ayt (v.)

ABHOR
ab HOR (v.)

ABRASIVE
ab RAY siv (adj.)

ABRIDGE
uh BRIJ (v.)

ABRUPT
ab RUPT (adj.)

ABSOLVE
ab ZOLV (v.)

loathe, detest

> Although Susan *abhorred* algebra because she felt it was too abstract, she was fond of geometry.

Synonyms: hate, dislike

to make shorter

> When the speaker saw that her time was running short, she decided to *abbreviate* her remarks.

Synonyms: shorten, reduce

to condense, shorten

> The teacher assigned an *abridged* version of the novel to her class, as the original was very long.

Synonyms: edit, condense

harsh and rough in manner

> Arnold threw the *abrasive* customer out of the store for bullying all the sales clerks.

Synonyms: rough, coarse

to forgive, free from blame

> The queen *absolved* the general from blame for the disastrous military campaign, much to his relief.

Synonyms: pardon, forgive

sudden; curt

> The lion was thrown off-guard by the *abrupt* change in direction of the elk herd.

Synonyms: unexpected, sudden

ACCOMPLICE
ah KOMP liss (n.)

ACCORD
uh KORD (v.)

ACQUIRE
ah KWIYR (v.)

ACRIMONY
AK ri MOW nee (n.)

ADEPT
ah DEPT (adj.)

ADORN
uh DORN (v.)

to bestow upon

Congress will *accord* him the Medal of Honor for his bravery in World War II.

Synonyms: award, confer

an associate in wrongdoing

Richard's *accomplice* in the prank was Tara, who watched out for witnesses while he performed the deed.

Synonyms: collaborator, accessory

bitterness, animosity

The ballgame ended in *acrimony* after the visiting team's pitcher hit three successive batters.

Synonyms: spite, rancor

to gain possession of

After this weekend's movie marathon, Lenora *acquired* a taste for Italian movies; she now wants to see all of them.

Synonyms: obtain, attain

to enhance or decorate

Tyler bought two more posters to *adorn* the walls of his room.

Synonyms: embellish, ornament

very skilled

After fifteen years of piano practice, Lisa became *adept* at playing songs without sheet music.

Synonyms: skillful, expert

AESTHETIC
ess THET ik (adj.)

AFFECTATION
ah feck TAY shun (n.)

AFFILIATION
ah FILL ee AY shun (n.)

AGGRESSIVE
uh GRESS iv (adj.)

AGILE
AH jel (adj.)

AGITATE
AH ji tayt (v.)

pretension; false display

In this day and age, wearing a high lace collar and a feathered hat to work is a rather bizarre *affectation*.

Synonyms: habit, mannerism

pertaining to beauty or art

The museum curator, with her fine *aesthetic* sense, created an exhibit that was a joy to behold.

Synonyms: visual, artistic

acts actively hostile; assertive, bold

While football may be an *aggressive* sport, off the field the captain of the team is a quiet guy.

Synonyms: forceful, assertive

an association to a group or organization

As a result of Diane's *affiliation* with the Dance Committee, she was ineligible to be chosen as Homecoming Queen.

Synonyms: association, connection

upset, disturb

Peter always cleans up his dorm room so it doesn't *agitate* his mother when she visits him.

Synonyms: stir up, rouse

well coordinated, nimble

The *agile* monkey leapt onto the table and snatched the boy's banana away in the blink of an eye.

Synonyms: supple, lithe

ALACRITY
ah LACK ri tee (adj.)

ALLEGATION
ah leh GAY shun (n.)

ALLEVIATE
ah LEE vee ayt (v.)

AMALGAMATION
ah MAL ga MAY shun (n.)

AMBIGUOUS
am BIG yoo us (n.)

AMBIVALENT
am BIV ah lent (adj.)

a claim without proof

The news reporter's *allegations* proved false after further investigation into the governor's conduct.

Synonyms: accusation, contention

cheerful willingness; speed

The eager dog obeyed with great *alacrity*, fetching the stick that had been tossed for him.

Synonyms: eagerness, enthusiasm

consolidation of smaller parts

The concert was an *amalgamation* of songs from different pop artists.

Synonyms: merger, union

to relieve, improve partially

This medicine will help to *alleviate* the pain.

Synonyms: ease, lessen

uncertain; emotionally conflicted

Wesley was *ambivalent* about Suni's request to get a dog.

Synonyms: unsure, undecided

uncertain; subject to multiple interpretations

The directions he gave were so *ambiguous* that we disagreed on which way to turn.

Synonyms: vague, unclear

AMIABLE
AYM ee uh bull (adj.)

AMICABLE
AM i ka bull (adj.)

AMORPHOUS
ah MOR fus (adj.)

AMPHITHEATER
AM fe thea ter (n.)

AMPLIFY
AM pleh fy (v.)

ANACHRONISTIC
uh NAK ru NISS tik (adj.)

friendly, agreeable

Despite their former arguments, the team was able to form an *amicable* working relationship.

Synonyms: good-natured, neighborly

friendly, pleasant, likable

The new boss was an *amiable* young man with a smile for everyone.

Synonyms: sociable, agreeable

arena theater with rising tiers around a central open space

The *amphitheater* in the park is the perfect place for a summer concert.

Synonyms: arena, auditorium

having no definite form

The movie *The Blob* featured an *amorphous* creature that was constantly changing shape.

Synonyms: formless, shapeless

from an incorrect or incongruous time period

The actor's appearance was amusingly *anachronistic* as he drove the modern automobile still dressed as a medieval peasant.

Synonyms: outdated, archaic

increase, intensify

We will need to *amplify* the music at the wedding so that everyone can hear it.

Synonyms: strengthen, magnify

ANALYZE
AN ah liyz (v.)

ANARCHIST
AN ar kist (n.)

ANCIENT
AYN shent (adj.)

ANECDOTE
AN ik dote (n.)

ANONYMOUS
uh NON uh muss (adj.)

ANTAGONIST
an TAG uh nist (n.)

one who aims for the overthrow of government

The *anarchist* organized a meeting to discuss ways to abolish the federal government.

Synonyms: revolutionary, rebel

to examine methodically

The forensics experts brought the blood back from the crime scene in order to *analyze* it in the lab.

Synonyms: study, investigate

story, usually funny account of an event

The child's grandparents entertained him for hours with *anecdotes* of their younger days.

Synonyms: tale, yarn

very old; antiquated

The curator at the museum was almost fooled into believing that a stone sculpture made last year was actually an *ancient* Greek statue.

Synonyms: antique

foe, opponent

In some comic books, the virtuous heroes are actually somewhat boring while their evil *antagonists* are considerably more compelling.

Synonyms: rival, adversary

of an unknown identity

Many newspaper sources remain *anonymous* so their bosses cannot fire them for giving information to the press.

Synonyms: nameless, unidentified

ARDOR
AR dur (n.)

ARID
AA rid (adj.)

ASCETIC
uh SET ik (adj.)

ASSERTION
uh SIR shun (n.)

ASSESS
uh SESS (v.)

ASSIDUOUS
uh SI joo iss (adj.)

extremely dry or deathly boring

The *arid* desert could produce no crops except those requiring very little water.

Synonyms: parched

great emotion

Bishop's *ardor* for scenic landscapes was evident when he passionately described the beauty of the Hudson Valley.

Synonyms: passion, enthusiasm

declaration, usually without proof

"Hillary's *assertion* that Shakespeare was a woman is totally false!" bellowed the irate professor.

Synonyms: claim, allegation

self-denying, abstinent

The monk lived an *ascetic* life deep in the wilderness, denying himself all forms of luxury.

Synonyms: austere

diligent, persistent, hard-working

The chauffer was *assiduous* in scrubbing the limousine, hoping to make a good impression on his employer.

Synonyms: industrious, diligent

to establish a value

After the car accident, the court sent a mechanic to *assess* the damage done by the defendant.

Synonyms: measure, gauge

ASSURANCE
uh SHOOR ans (n.)

ASTUTE
uh STOOT (adj.)

ASYLUM
uh SY lum (n.)

ATTAIN
uh TAYN (v.)

ATYPICAL
ay TIP ih kul (adj.)

AUDACIOUS
aw DAY shis (adj.)

having good judgment

> The novelist Judy Blume is an *astute* judge of human nature; her characters ring true.

Synonyms: shrewd, perceptive

guarantee

> Roger and Joelle gave their *assurance* to their parents that they would be home in time for their curfew.

Synonyms: promise, pledge

to accomplish, gain

> It is clear that Clem's hard work will help him *attain* that raise he's been hoping for.

Synonyms: reach, achieve

a place offering protection and safety

> Many of the immigrants to the United States in the early part of the twentieth century sought *asylum* from government persecution in their home countries.

Synonyms: refuge, haven

bold, fearless

> The protestors' *audacious* slogans angered the large corporation with their sharp critiques, but also won considerable attention and support from onlookers.

Synonyms: daring, brave

unusual, irregular

> It was *atypical* of Patrick to forget his lunch; he almost always remembered to take it.

Synonyms: uncommon

BALK
BAWK (v.)

BANALITY
buh NAL ih tee (n.)

BANE
BAYN (n.)

BANISH
BAN ish (v.)

BARD
BARD (n.)

BARRICADE
BAR ih kayd (n.)

the quality of being trite, commonplace

All the critics complained about the *banality* of the movie last night—it had a completely predictable and inane plot.

Synonyms: predictability

to refuse, shirk; prevent

The horse *balked* at jumping over the high fence and instead threw his rider off.

Synonyms: cringe, recoil

drive away, expel

After his defeat at Waterloo, the European leaders chose to *banish* Napoleon to the remote island of Elba.

Synonyms: exile, send away

cause of harm or ruin; source of annoyance

Speeches were the *bane* of Jenny's existence; she hated having to stand up in front of a crowd.

Synonyms: nuisance, pest

obstacle, barrier

During the French Revolution, students set up *barricades* in Paris to keep the army from moving through the streets.

Synonyms: blockade

lyrical poet

Bards in medieval times were usually illiterate and so memorized incredibly long tales and songs.

Synonyms: poet, writer

BENIGN
bi NIYN (adj.)

BEQUEATH
bi KWEETH (v.)

BERATE
bee RAYT (v.)

BEREFT
Be REFT (adj.)

BETRAY
be TRAY (v.)

BEWILDER
be WILL der (v.)

pass on, hand down

Fred thought that his grandmother was penniless and so was shocked when she *bequeathed* to him a beautiful gold watch.

Synonyms: leave, bestow

gentle, harmless

Although many children in the neighborhood feared the old dog, he was actually quite *benign* and never even barked.

Synonyms: kind, benevolent

deprived of something

The reality television show was *bereft* of anything resembling wit or intelligence.

Synonyms: lacking

to scold harshly

After the class's dismal performance on the exam, Professor Wilson *berated* everyone for their laziness and lack of preparation.

Synonyms: rebuke, scold

to confuse or puzzle

The class found themselves *bewildered* by Professor Yasmeet's lecture on advanced photonics.

Synonyms: baffle, perplex

to be false or disloyal to

Unable to withstand the power of the dark side of the force, Darth Vader *betrayed* his teacher's confidence.

Synonyms: deceive, let down

BIASED

BY ust (adj.)

BILK

BILK (v.)

BLAZE

BLAYZ (v.)

BLEMISH

BLEM ish (n.)

BOAST

BOHST (v.)

BOON

BOON (n.)

to defraud, swindle

Several lawyers were caught *bilking* clients out of millions of dollars in an illegal real estate scheme.

Synonyms: trick, con

prejudiced

The defendant's lawyer filed a motion to move the case to a new town because the people in this one were all *biased* against her client.

Synonyms: unfair, partial

imperfection, flaw

"Even models have *blemishes*!" remarked the make-up artist as she liberally applied foundation.

Synonyms: mark, fault

shine brightly, flare up suddenly

The fire *blazed* through the night, providing heat and light to the campers as they slept.

Synonyms: radiate, glow

blessing, something to be thankful for

The oasis in the desert was a *boon* to us after a week of wandering.

Synonyms: benefit, advantage

speak with excessive pride

"I can beat all of you at that video game any day of the week," *boasted* Derrick last night, right before an unprecedented losing streak.

Synonyms: brag, show off

CACOPHONY
ke KOF o nee (n.)

CADENCE
KAYD ns (n.)

CAJOLE
ka JOL (v.)

CALAMITY
ka LAM uh tee (n.)

CALCULATING
KAL kyu lay ting (adj.)

CALUMNY
KAL um nee (n.)

rhythmic flow; marching beat

Perhaps because he was also an accomplished musician, Pierre spoke with a lovely *cadence*, enchanting all of his listeners.

Synonyms: tempo, beat

jarring, unpleasant noise

The junior high orchestra created an almost unbearable *cacophony* as they tried to tune their instruments.

Synonyms: dissonance, disharmony

disaster, catastrophe

Last year's formal dance was a *calamity*: the band was an hour late, and the food was spoiled.

Synonyms: tragedy

flatter, persuade

The spoiled girl could *cajole* her father into buying her anything.

Synonyms: coax, wheedle

false and malicious accusation, misrepresentation

The unscrupulous politician used *calumny* to bring down his opponent in the senatorial race.

Synonyms: slander, defamation

shrewd, crafty

The *calculating* lawyer put the mother of his client on the witness stand in order to garner sympathy.

Synonyms: scheming, cunning

CEREBRAL
suh REE brell (adj.)

CHALLENGE
CHAL enj (v.)

CHAPPED
CHAP d (adj.)

CHERISH
CHER ish (v.)

CIRCUITOUS
sir KYOO ih tuss (adj.)

CIRCUMLOCUTION
SIR kuhm low KYOO shin (n.)

take exception to, call into question

As soon as the new CEO began working, he set up policies and goals that *challenged* the way the company had been operating for the past twenty years.

Synonyms: dispute, contest

intellectual

Though a star athlete, Paul defied stereotypes by reading difficult books, playing chess, and engaging in other *cerebral* pursuits.

Synonyms: intellectual, rational

to remember fondly, treat with affection

Despite the fact that Esther and Lily have barely had a chance to talk since college, they will always *cherish* their deep childhood friendship.

Synonyms: treasure, value

cracked or reddened by cold or exposure

After cycling through heavy winter winds all day, Sean's lips and cheeks were severely *chapped*.

Synonyms: rough, dry

roundabout, lengthy way of saying something

He avoided discussing the real issues with endless *circumlocutions*.

Synonyms: wordiness, longwindedness

indirect, taking the longest route

The cab driver took a *circuitous* route to the airport, making me miss my plane.

Synonyms: roundabout, meandering

CLICHÉ
klee SHAY (n.)

CLIENTELE
kly en TELL (n.)

CLIQUE
KLIK (n.)

CLOYING
KLOY ing (adj.)

CLUTTERED
KLUT erd (adj.)

COGNIZANT
KOG ni zent (adj.)

body of customers or patrons

Le Caravelle, one of the most expensive restaurants in the city, caters to a wealthy clientele.

Synonyms: clients

overused expression or idea

Audiences moaned audibly during the movie as the characters kept repeating clichés instead of saying anything new or interesting.

Synonyms: truism, formula

overly sweet

Television viewers today find the cloying shows of the 1950s like Leave it to Beaver to be too unrealistic for their tastes.

Synonyms: sugary, syrupy

small exclusive group

Roberto's clique, the most fashionable group of students in the school, refused to associate with any other students.

Synonyms: faction

fully informed, conscious

Principal Davies kept posting signs around the school about the new dress code until he was sure that the students were cognizant of the changed regulations.

Synonyms: aware, mindful

messy, disorderly

Jeffrey could no longer manage working in such a cluttered environment, so he spent half the day cleaning up the mess around his office.

Synonyms: jumbled, chaotic

COHERENT
ko HEE rent (adj.)

COHESION
ko HEE zhun (n.)

COLLABORATOR
ko LAB u RAY tor (n.)

COLLAGE
ko LAZH (n.)

COLLOQUIAL
ka LOW kwee al (adj.)

COLLUSION
ku LOO zhen (n.)

act or state of sticking together; close union

Under its new leadership, the team's *cohesion* of spirit led them to believe they could win the championship game.

Synonyms: unity, consistency

intelligible, lucid, understandable

Cathy was so tired that her speech was barely *coherent*.

Synonyms: rational, articulate

assemblage of diverse elements

Dean Wintner used a *collage* of newspaper clippings to decorate the wall of her office.

Synonyms: collection

someone who helps on a task

Lucy was Chuck's *collaborator* on the file; he did the research, and she wrote the briefs.

Synonyms: colleague, partner

collaboration, complicity

The Mayor denied any *collusion* even after members of his staff were discovered to be corrupt.

Synonyms: conspiracy, involvement

characteristic of informal speech

The book was written in *colloquial* style so that the information in it would be more user-friendly.

Synonyms: idiomatic, conversational

COMPASSION
kum PASH in (n.)

COMPELLING
kom PELL ing (adj.)

COMPENSATE
KOMP en sayt (v.)

COMPLACENCE
kom PLAY senss (n.)

COMPLEMENT
KOMP leh ment (v.)

COMPLEX
kom PLEKS (adj.)

urgently requiring attention, forceful

"Although the plaintiff has offered *compelling* evidence of wrongdoing by the defendant," said the seasoned judge, "I have no choice but to side with the defense in this matter."

Synonyms: convincing, persuasive

sympathy, helpfulness or mercy

In a touching show of *compassion*, the little girl presented the grieving widow with a flower.

Synonyms: empathy, concern

self-satisfaction, lack of concern

The artist's growing *complacence* was surprising, since her early work was characterized by exacting attention to detail and ruthless self-critique.

Synonyms: satisfaction, smugness

to repay

The moving company *compensated* me for the broken furniture.

Synonyms: recompense, reimburse

intricate, complicated

Critics hailed J.R.R. Tolkien for creating a *complex* and complete world within the framework of a popular novel.

Synonyms: multifaceted, dense

to complete or perfect

Gina's pink sweater *complemented* her red hair perfectly.

Synonyms: set off, match

CONCEITED
kon SEET id (adj.)

CONCEIVABLE
kon SEEV uh bull (adj.)

CONCILIATORY
kon SILL ee ah tory (adj.)

CONCOCT
kon KOKT (v.)

CONCORDANT
kon KOR dint (adj.)

CONDEMNATION
kon dem NAY shun (n.)

capable of being understood or imagined

It's *conceivable* that technology will advance to a point at which cars will drive themselves.

Synonyms: possible. plausible

holding an unduly high opinion of oneself, vain

The author was too *conceited* to acknowledge that any revision to the novel was necessary.

Synonyms: self important

to devise, using skill and intelligence

When pressed for an excuse for his weeklong absence, Richard *concocted* a story so outrageous that his teacher knew he was lying.

Synonyms: make up, invent

overcoming distrust or hostility

Fred made the *conciliatory* gesture of buying Abby flowers after their big fight.

Synonyms: appeasing, pacifying

an expression of strong disapproval

The president's *condemnation* of the scandal followed allegations that he himself had been involved.

Synonyms: censure, blame

harmonious, agreeing

Bruce, *concordant* with his mother's wishes, didn't follow his friends to the rally.

Synonyms: in accord, agreeable

CONFIGURATION
kon fig yu RAY shun (n.)

CONFIRM
kon FIRM (v.)

CONFISCATION
kon fis KAY shun (n.)

CONFLICT
KON flikt (n.)

CONFORMITY
kon FORM ih tee (n.)

CONFOUND
kun FOWND (v.)

verify

Many airlines require their passengers to call a day in advance and *confirm* their reservation for the flight.

Synonyms: corroborate, bear out

arrangement of parts or elements

Each year's yearbook centerfold has the class in a different *configuration*; this year they are arranged to spell out "SENIORS."

Synonyms: pattern

a clash, a battle

The *conflict* between Debbie and Gerry heightened as the former friends began to insult each other publicly.

Synonyms: disagreement, quarrel

seizure by authorities

The *confiscation* of Bethany's cell phone was the first step in a campaign to stop students from calling each other during class.

Synonyms: taking away

to baffle, perplex

Vince, *confounded* by the difficult algebra problems, threw his math book at the wall in utter frustration.

Synonyms: confuse, puzzle

similarity in form or character

Bruce acted in *conformity* with the rules set down by the governing board of the school; he was not one to act up.

Synonyms: consistency, accord

CONFRONTATIONAL
kon fron TAY shun al (adj.)

CONGEAL
kun JEEL (v.)

CONSECRATE
KON si krayt (v.)

CONSENSUS
kon SEN suss (n.)

CONSERVATISM
kon SER va tizm (n.)

CONSERVE
kon SERV (v.)

to become thick, as a liquid freezing

The melted butter *congealed* in the container after a few minutes in the refrigerator.

Synonyms: solidify, coagulate

eager to defy, especially in a face-to-face encounter

Known by his coworkers to be *confrontational*, J.B. was elected to discuss the upcoming budget cuts with the company's president.

Synonyms: challenging, provoking

unanimity, agreement of opinion or attitude

The jurors finally reached a *consensus* and declared the defendant guilty as charged.

Synonyms: accord

to declare sacred; dedicate to a goal

The priest *consecrated* the marriage under the cover of night, fearing that the long standing family dispute would prevent the couple from taking their vows.

Synonyms: sanctify, bless

use sparingly; protect from loss or harm

The government urged citizens to *conserve* water in the midst of the drought.

Synonyms: preserve, save

inclination to maintain traditional rules

The governor favored *conservatism* in government and chose not to reexamine many of the long-standing statutes.

Synonyms: tradition, convention

CONSOLATION
kon so LAY shun (n.)

CONSTELLATION
kon stuh LAY shun (n.)

CONSUMMATE
KON suh mit (adj.)

CONSUMPTION
kon SUMP shun (n.)

CONTAGIOUS
kon TAY jus (adj.)

CONTAMINATE
kon TAM uh nayt (v.)

a collection of stars with a perceived design

>Some astrologers believe that the placement of different *constellations* in the sky affects one's luck at a given time.

Synonym: group of stars

something providing comfort for a loss or hardship

>The ample inheritance offered little *consolation* to the grief-stricken widow.

Synonyms: solace

the act of eating or taking in

>Many teachers prohibit the *consumption* of food and drink during class because it disrupts the other students.

Synonyms: intake, ingestion

accomplished, complete, perfect

>The skater delivered a *consummate* performance, perfect in every aspect.

Synonyms: ideal, flawless

to make impure by contact

>The scientists had to wear special rubber suits when working in the lab so they wouldn't *contaminate* the delicate solution.

Synonyms: pollute, taint

spreading from one to another

>Lucy was ordered by the doctor to stay home until her disease was no longer *contagious*.

Synonyms: infectious, communicable

CONTRITE

kon TRYT (adj.)

CONTROVERSIAL

kon tro VER shul (adj.)

CONUNDRUM

ka NUN drum (n.)

CONVENIENT

kon VEEN yent (adj.)

CONVENTION

kon VEN shen (n.)

CONVENTIONAL

kon VEN sheh null (adj.)

producing or marked by heated dispute

Many people were very upset by the *controversial* increase in gasoline taxes that the government has authorized.

Synonyms: contentious, devisive

deeply sorrowful and repentant for a wrong

While Max appeared *contrite* before the court and even shed tears, the judge showed no leniency at the sentencing.

Synonyms: remorseful, sorry

favorable to one's comfort or needs

The hardest part about working with a big group is finding a time that is *convenient* for everyone.

Synonyms: expedient, opportune

riddle or problem with no solution

The man puzzled over the *conundrum* for hours, but eventually gave up in despair.

Synonyms: mystery

typical, customary, commonplace

Conventional wisdom holds that hard work and honesty pay off in the end.

Synonyms: usual, normal

general acceptance of practices or attitudes

It's important when writing essays and letters to always follow the *conventions* of standard written English.

Synonyms: standard, custom

CONVERGENCE
kun VER jinss (n.)

CONVEY
kon VAY (v.)

CONVICT
kon VICT (v.)

CONVICTION
kon VIC shin (n.)

CONVOLUTED
KON vuh loo tid (adj.)

CORDIAL
KOR jel (adj.)

to transport; to make known

The goal of the game is to *convey* a phrase to your teammates without using words.

Synonyms: express, communicate

the state of separate elements joining or coming together

No one in the quiet neighborhood could have predicted the mass *convergence* of artists, writers, and musicians and the birth of a miniature renaissance.

Synonyms: junction, union

fixed or strong belief

Sally would not be swayed from her *conviction* that the best color for a sports car is red.

Synonyms: principle, strong opinion

to find guilty of a crime

If the jury chooses to *convict* the defendant, the attorney will appeal to a higher court.

Synonyms: condemn

warm and sincere, friendly

"How have you been, Walt?" exclaimed Matthew as he extended his arm for a *cordial* handshake.

Synonyms: pleasant, affable

twisted, complicated, involved

Although many people bought the well-known philosopher's text, few could follow its *convoluted* ideas and theories.

Synonyms: elaborate, complex

CRASS
KRASS (adj.)

CREDO
KREE doh (n.)

CRESCENDO
kruh SHEN do (n.)

CRUDE
KROOD (adj.)

CUE
KYOO (n.)

CULPABLE
KUL puh bull (adj.)

system of principles or beliefs

> When doctors took the Hippocratic oath, they promised to follow the *credo* "first, do no harm."

Synonyms: philosophy, doctrine

crude, unrefined

> Miss Manner watched in horror as her *crass* date belched loudly and snapped his fingers at the waiter.

Synonyms: insensitive, tactless

unrefined, natural; blunt, offensive

> After two months of ignoring Billy's *crude* remarks, Denise finally told him that his comments were offensive to women.

Synonyms: coarse, vulgar

gradual increase in volume, force, or intensity

> When the orchestra reached the *crescendo* of the symphony, the conductor was waving his arms around wildly.

Synonyms: loudening, upsurge

guilty, responsible for wrong

> The CEO is *culpable* for the company's bankruptcy, as the beginning of his new initiatives marked the end of profits.

Synonyms: liable, to blame

reminder, prompting

> Sally nervously sat backstage waiting for the director to give her the *cue* to start singing.

Synonyms: signal, sign

DANGLE
DANG gul (v.)

DATED
DAY tid (adj.)

DAUNTING
DAWN ting (adj.)

DEBACLE
di BAK ul (n.)

DEBASE
de BAYS (v.)

DEBILITATING
dee BIL uh tay ting (adj.)

out of style

> Though she was flattered at inheriting the gown, she secretly thought it might be a bit *dated* for a modern wedding.

Synonyms: passé, old-fashioned

to hang loosely

> The trainer *dangled* a treat above the nose of the obedient puppy.

Synonyms: swing

disastrous collapse, total failure

> The team's certain victory somehow transformed into a complete *debacle* as they made countless errors and failed to communicate.

Synonyms: fiasco, catastrophe

discouraging

> While running the New York Marathon may be a *daunting* task to some, the event consistently draws thousands of participants.

Synonyms: intimidating

impairing the strength or energy

> The company's relocation was *debilitating* to its employees; they lost all will to work in their new environment.

Synonyms: incapacitating, devastating

to degrade or lower in quality or stature

> The president's deceitful actions *debased* his office.

Synonyms: humiliate, demean

DEFT
DEFT (adj.)

DEGRADATION
deg ruh DAY shun (n.)

DELEGATE
DEL uh gayt (v.)

DELETE
de LEET (v.)

DELETERIOUS
de le TEER ee us (adj.)

DELIBERATION
de lib uh RAY shun (n.)

reduction in worth or dignity

Sally's *degradation* was on display for the whole school when she was replaced as captain of the varsity team.

Synonyms: humiliation, disgrace

skillful, dexterous

The potter used her *deft* touch to demonstrate how to make a perfectly shaped bowl.

Synonyms: adroit

remove

After numerous phone calls from a telemarketing company, we called to have our name *deleted* from their list.

Synonyms: erase

to give powers to another

A good leader knows when to *delegate* tasks to others and when to handle an issue directly.

Synonyms: designate, appoint

discussion or careful consideration of an issue

The jury's *deliberations* took several days; they felt the gravity of the decision they had to make and wanted to make sure they did the right thing.

Synonyms: reflection, thought

destructive, detrimental

Environmentalists are trying to make it illegal to dump *deleterious* substances into lakes and wildlife reserves.

Synonyms: injurious, harmful

DESOLATE
DES uh lit (adj.)

DESPOTISM
DES puh tizm (n.)

DESTITUTION
des tih TOO shun (n.)

DETERMINE
di TUR min (v.)

DETRACTOR
di TRAK tur (n.)

DEVASTATE
DEV uh stayt (v.)

dominance through threat of violence

Unwilling to resort to the *despotism* of past rulers, the king granted unprecedented freedom to his people when they threatened to revolt.

Synonyms: tyranny, autocracy

deserted, lifeless, barren

The *desolate* landscape in the desert left the group hungry for the plush greenery of their hometown.

Synonyms: isolated, uninhabited

to decide, establish

The scientists were unable to *determine* the cause of the strange ailment.

Synonyms: find out, ascertain

complete poverty

The *destitution* of certain parts of the state has only begun to be addressed by the governor.

Synonyms: penury, impoverishment

destroy; overwhelm, stun

Paul was *devastated* by the team's loss in the championship game.

Synonyms: destroy, wreck

one who belittles something else

The president's *detractors* noted that, although well-written, the address was definitely penned by a professional speechwriter.

Synonyms: critic, heckler

DIGRESSION
di GRESH un (n.)

DILATORY
DIL uh tor ee (adj.)

DIMINISH
di MIN ish (v.)

DINGY
DIN jee (adj.)

DISAVOW
dis uh VOW (v.)

DISCERN
di SURN (v.)

tending to delay

The senator used *dilatory* measures in order to keep the bill from appearing before Congress.

Synonyms: slow, tardy

the act of straying, an instance of straying

The number of *digressions* from the main point of the discussion made the lecture difficult to follow.

Synonyms: aside, deviation

shabby, drab

Penelope thought her new apartment looked a little *dingy*, but she was sure a fresh coat of paint would brighten it up.

Synonyms: dirty, discolored

to make smaller

Despite all the advances in modern medicine, doctors have been unable to *diminish* people's susceptibility to many diseases.

Synonyms: reduce, weaken

to perceive something obscure

It is easy to *discern* the difference between real butter and butter-flavored topping.

Synonyms: understand, detect

to refuse to acknowledge

Despite claims by his critics that he knew of the impending invasion, the king *disavowed* any prior knowledge of the attack.

Synonyms: disown, renounce

DISCOURSE
DIS kors (n.)

DISCOURTEOUS
dis KUR tee us (adj.)

DISCREDIT
diss KRED it (v.)

DISCREPANCY
dis KREP un see (n.)

DISCRETION
dis KRESH in (n.)

DISCRETIONARY
dis KRESH in er ee (adj.)

rude

Sarah's parents, disturbed by the *discourteous* manner in which their daughter's boyfriend addressed them, promptly sent him away.

Synonyms: impolite

verbal exchange, conversation

The first step in the trade negotiations was starting a *discourse* between the two participants so they could discuss common goals.

Synonyms: dialogue, discussion

difference between

The obvious *discrepancy* between Carl's poor participation in class and brilliant paper led the teacher to believe he had been helped.

Synonyms: inconsistency, incongruity

to harm the reputation of

Unfortunately, in today's political arena, more time is spent trying to *discredit* one's opponents than discussing the actual issues.

Synonyms: dishonor, disgrace

subject to one's own judgment

Ambassadors have some *discretionary* powers, though they must bow to the authority of the secretary of state.

Synonyms: flexible, unrestricted

ability to judge on one's own

Rather than try to make unilateral decisions for the entire company, the president let the store managers use their own *discretion* when deciding how many employees to hire.

Synonyms: judgment, discrimination

DISPARATE
dis PAR it (adj.)

DISPEL
dis PELL (v.)

DISPLAY
dis PLAY (v.)

DISPUTANT
dis PYOO tent (n.)

DISREGARD
dis rih GARD (v.)

DISSEMBLE
dih SEM bul (v.)

to drive out or scatter

Arnie's heroic rescue of the family from the flames *dispelled* any doubts that he could be a good fireman.

Synonyms: dismiss, disperse

dissimilar, different in kind

Although the twins are virtually identical physically, their personalities are *disparate*.

Synonyms: unalike

someone in an argument

When Mr. Walters entered and heard the yelling, he immediately ran over and separated the two *disputants*.

Synonyms: fighter, combatant

to show, to exhibit, to present

Unwilling to *display* her artwork to the public, Sandra kept most of her paintings in her room for only friends and family to see.

Synonyms: show, exhibit

to pretend, disguise one's motives

The villain could *dissemble* no longer; he finally confessed the forgery to the police.

Synonyms: evade, hedge

to give no attention

The building manager knew that people were going to *disregard* the "Do Not Enter" sign, so he put a security guard in front of the broken elevator.

Synonyms: ignore, discount

DIVERT

di VURT (v.)

DIVINATION

div uh NAY shin (n.)

DIVISIVE

dih VIY siv (adj.)

DIVULGE

di VULJ (v.)

DOGMATIC

dog MAT ik (adj.)

DOMINANT

DOM uh nent (adj.)

foretelling the future using supernatural means

Madame Culova claimed to be an expert in *divination*, reading palms, tea leaves, and crystal balls.

Synonyms: prediction, forecast

to turn aside, to distract

To keep the child quiet during the doctor's examination, the nurse *diverted* his attention with puppets.

Synonyms: side track

to make known

Pat was fired for *divulging* company secrets to its competitors.

Synonyms: reveal, disclose

creating disunity or conflict

The leader used *divisive* tactics to pit his enemies against each other.

Synonyms: discordant, disruptive

most prominent, exercising the most control

The *dominant* reasons for the company's relocation were the cheaper rent and larger workforce.

Synonyms: leading, main

rigidly fixed in opinion, opinionated

I can appreciate the philosopher's earlier work, but late in life he became excessively *dogmatic* and abandoned his initial open-mindedness.

Synonyms: inflexible, unbending

EBB
EBB (v.)

ECCENTRIC
ek SEN trik (adj.)

ECLECTIC
ee KLEK tik (adj.)

ECSTASY
EK stuh see (n.)

ELOQUENT
EL uh kwent (adj.)

EFFICACIOUS
ef ih KAY shus (adj.)

abnormal, unconventional

Belinda thought her aunt was a bit *eccentric*: she insisted on taking her cat everywhere.

Synonyms: odd, peculiar

to fade away, recede

From her beachside balcony, Melissa enjoyed watching the tide *ebb* and flow.

Synonyms: diminish, fade

intense joy or delight

Joan was in *ecstasy* when she discovered that she would be traveling to Europe for the summer.

Synonyms: elation, bliss

made up of elements from different sources

Roberta always had an *eclectic* taste in music; she enjoyed listening to both rap and opera daily.

Synonyms: assorted, diverse

efficient

Penicillin was one of the most *efficacious* drugs on the market when it was first introduced; the drug completely eliminated almost all bacterial infections for which it was administered.

Synonyms: effective, sucessful

strongly expressing emotion

Sean, discussing a topic very dear to him, addressed the room with a vivid, *eloquent* speech.

EMBITTERED

em BIT urd (adj.)

EMEND
ih MEND (v.)

EMIGRATE

EM ih grayt (v.)

EMISSARY
EM ih ser ee (n.)

EMOLLIENT

ih MOL yent (adj.)

EMPATHY

EM pu thee (n.)

to correct a text

The catalog was *emended* so the correct prices were given for the products on sale.

Synonyms: revise, alter

resentful, cynical

Gregory was *embittered* after ten years of working at the same job with no promotion or raise.

Synonyms: disillusioned, sour

an agent sent as a representative

The President's *emissaries* were instructed not to discuss their mission with anyone other than the Prime Minister.

Synonyms: envoy, agent

to leave one country to live in another

When the potato famine hit Ireland, many families were forced to leave their homes and *emigrate* to the United States.

Synonyms: live elsewhere

identification with the feelings of others

Having taught English herself, Julie felt a strong *empathy* for the troubled English teacher in the film.

Synonyms: understanding, sympathy

having soothing qualities, especially for skin

After using the *emollient* lotion for a couple of weeks, Donna's skin changed from scaly to smooth.

Synonyms: soothing

EMPHATIC
em FAT ik (adj.)

EMULATE
EM yoo layt (v.)

ENCHANT
en CHANT (v.)

ENCOMPASS
en COM pass (v.)

ENCROACH
en KROHCH (v.)

ENDEMIC
en DEM ik (adj.)

to imitate

The son sought to *emulate* his father in every way possible; he joined the same clubs and studied for the same jobs.

Synonyms: follow, copy

forceful and definite

When asked if they wanted to come to school over the weekends, the class answered with an *emphatic* "NO!"

Synonyms: categorical, ardent

to constitute, encircle

The syllabus for Professor Grumman's upcoming course will *encompass* all American political history from Teddy Roosevelt to FDR.

Synonyms: include, cover

attract and delight

Lorna was dazzled by her first visit to the Museum of Modern Art; the brilliant colors and bold paintings *enchanted* her.

Synonyms: charm, captivate

belonging to a particular area

The health department determined that the outbreak was *endemic* to the small village, so they quarantined the inhabitants before the virus could spread.

Synonyms: local, inherent

to impinge, infringe, intrude upon

Some environmentalists are concerned that as the human population expands, we continually *encroach* on natural habitats like the rainforests.

Synonyms: invade, trespass

ENDORSE
en DORSS (v.)

ENDURANCE
en DOOR uns (n.)

ENDURE
en DYOOR (v.)

ENDURING
en DYOOR ing (adj.)

ENERVATE
EN er vayt (v.)

ENFORCE
en FORS (v.)

ability to withstand hardships

> To prepare for the marathon, Becky built up her *endurance* by running ten miles every day.

Synonyms: staying power, fortitude

to give approval to, sanction

> The politician refused to *endorse* any group that wouldn't grant equal rights to all people.

Synonyms: support, approve

lasting, continuing

> Isaac Newton has established an *enduring* legacy that continues even today as millions of students begin their studies of physics with his three laws that describe motion.

Synonyms: durable, long-term

carry on despite hardships

> Skiing is an exciting and invigorating sport for those who can *endure* being out in the cold all day.

Synonyms: bear, tolerate

to compel others to adhere or observe

> While it is the job of the legislative branch of government to create the laws, it is the job of the executive branch to *enforce* them.

Synonyms: implement, impose

to weaken, sap strength from

> The guerillas hoped that a series of surprise attacks would *enervate* the regular army.

Synonyms: debilitate, weaken

ENFRANCHISE
en FRAN chiyz (v.)

ENHANCE
in HANSS (v.)

ENIGMATIC
en ig MAT ik (adj.)

ENMITY
EN mi tee (n.)

ENORMOUS
ee NOR muss (adj.)

ENSEMBLE
on SOM bul (n.)

to improve, bring to a greater level of intensity

They can sure use a hand in *enhancing* the quality of the food in the cafeteria.

Synonyms: augment, add to

to give the right to vote to

American women were not *enfranchised* until the ratification of the Nineteenth Amendment in 1920.

Synonyms: right to vote

antagonism, ill will

The *enmity* between the rival families continued for hundreds of years.

Synonyms: bad feeling, hostility

puzzling

The professor's *enigmatic* answers to the questions about the upcoming exam left the class more confused than they had been earlier.

Synonyms: mysterious, inscrutable

group of parts that contribute to a whole single effect

Everyone admired Louis's *ensemble* as he came into work today; his hat and suit made him look like a character in an old detective movie.

Synonyms: collection, assembly

very great in size or degree

The *enormous* sculpture of the elephant dwarfed the delighted children.

Synonyms: huge, massive

ERADICATE
ih RAD ih kayt (v.)

ERASURE
i RAY shur (n.)

EROSION
ih ROW zhin (n.)

ERRATIC
ih RAT ik (adj.)

ERRONEOUS
ih ROWN ee us (adj.)

ESPOUSE
eh SPOWZ (v.)

the act or instance of erasing

Dave's *erasure* from the company database was performed as soon as he was fired, so he was unable to return to the office building that same afternoon.

Synonyms: removal, crossing out

to erase or wipe out

It is unlikely that poverty will ever be completely *eradicated* in this country, though the general standard of living has significantly improved in recent decades.

Synonyms: eliminate, destroy

unpredictable, inconsistent

Many directors refused to work with the famous comedian because his *erratic* behavior made them nervous.

Synonyms: unreliable, irregular

the process or condition of wearing away

When we bought our beach house ten years ago, it was half a mile from the water, but *erosion* has shortened the beach so we are now considerably closer.

Synonyms: corrosion, wearing down

to support or advocate

The vice-president could not *espouse* the plot to fire the store manager.

Synonyms: adopt, promote

mistaken, inaccurate

Instead of methodically analyzing the outcomes of the experiment, the group constantly jumped to *erroneous* conclusions about the results.

Synonyms: flawed, wrong

EVALUATE
ee VAL yoo ayt (v.)

EVANESCENT
ev in ESS nt (adj.)

EVAPORATE
ee VAP uh rayt (v.)

EVENHANDED
ee ven HAND id (adj.)

EXACERBATE
ig ZAS ur bayt (v.)

EXACTING
eg ZAK ting (adj.)

momentary, transient, short-lived

Her moment of fame proved *evanescent,* as she quickly vanished from the public view.

Synonyms: fleeting, passing

to examine or judge carefully

The judge instructed the jury to carefully *evaluate* all the evidence before coming to a conclusion.

Synonyms: assess, appraise

fair, impartial

Both lawyers respected the judge for his *evenhanded* treatment of the case.

Synonyms: unbiased, neutral

to vanish quickly

You need to watch the pot carefully, since once the water *evaporates,* the sauce will begin to burn.

Synonyms: fade, disappear

requiring a lot of care or attention

Baking bread is an *exacting* task, since air temperature and humidity are as important to the final product as the precise blend of ingredients.

Synonyms: demanding, challenging

to aggravate, intensify the bad qualities of

It is unwise to take aspirin to relieve heartburn; instead of providing relief, the drug will only *exacerbate* the problem.

Synonyms: worsen

EXCURSION
ek SKUHR zhen (n.)

EXEMPLARY
egg ZEM pluh ree (adj.)

EXEMPLIFY
eg ZEMP lih fiy (v.)

EXHAUST
eg ZOST (v.)

EXHORTATION
eg zor TAY shun (n.)

EXORBITANT
eg ZORB ih tant (adj.)

outstanding, an example to others

His *exemplary* behavior was a model for the rest of the class.

Synonyms: consummate, excellent

short journey, usually for pleasure

Billy followed James on his *excursions* to the park trying to understand why bird watching so excited him.

Synonyms: outing, jaunt

to wear out; use up completely

Advocates of solar power claim that continuing our current rate of oil consumption will *exhaust* the world's resources in the near future.

Synonyms: tire out, drain

to show by example

Mark Twain's stories *exemplify* his ability to portray the common man with both humor and pathos.

Synonyms: demonstrate

extravagant, greater than reasonable

After freezing temperatures destroyed the harvest, shops charged *exorbitant* prices for oranges.

Synonyms: inflated, excessive

speech that advises or pleads

The minister's *exhortation* convinced the king to show mercy to his enemies and spare their lives.

Synonyms: appeal, plea

EXPEDITE
EK spe diyt (v.)

EXPERTISE
ek spur TEEZ (n.)

EXPLANATORY
ek SPLAN uh tor ee (adj.)

EXPLOIT
ek SPLOYT (v.)

EXPROPRIATE
ek SPRO pree ayt (v.)

EXPURGATE
EK spur gayt (v.)

knowledge in a particular area

In questions about grammar, I usually defer to Eileen; her *expertise* in the area outweighs my own.

Synonyms: know-how, skill

to speed up the progress of

The lawyers worked judiciously to *expedite* the release of their client from prison.

Synonyms: accelerate

take advantage of

The brilliant tactician studied his enemy's methods to discover a weakness that he could easily *exploit* in battle.

Synonyms: use, manipulate

serving to make clear

Before going into detail about her project, Leeann wrote an *explanatory* section to outline her ideas.

Synonyms: clarifying, descriptive

to censor

Government propagandists *expurgated* all negative references to the dictator from the film.

Synonyms: repress

forcibly take one's property

Historically, feudal lords *expropriated* the landowners who refused to pay taxes.

Synonyms: confiscate, impound

EXTRAVAGANT
ek STRAV uh gent (adj.)

EXTREME
ek STREEM (adj.)

EXTRICATE
EK stri kayt (v.)

EXTROVERTED
EK stro ver tid (adj.)

EXULTANT
eg ZUL tent (adj.)

FABRICATED
fab rih KAY tid (adj.)

very intense, of the greatest severity

When the army officer discovered that his unit was getting lazy, he took *extreme* measures to get them back into shape, instituting mandatory weight training and early morning runs.

Synonyms: radical, immoderate

lavish; unreasonably high, exorbitant

Among other *extravagant* demands, the touring rock band insisted on a specific brand of bottled water in their dressing rooms.

Synonyms: excessive, overdone

outgoing, easily talks to others

Cynthia, the most *extroverted* student in the class, was the popular frontrunner for president.

Synonyms: demonstrative, talkative

to free from, disentangle

The fly was unable to *extricate* itself from the spider's web.

Synonyms: extract, free

constructed, invented; faked, falsified

The reporter was disgraced when it was uncovered that the stories he'd published were largely *fabricated*.

Synonyms: made-up, fictitious

triumphant

The *exultant* investor cheered gleefully as he watched his stock prices skyrocket.

Synonyms: jubilant, elated

FATHOM
FAH thom (v.)

FAVORITISM
FAV uh rih tizm (n.)

FEIGN
FAYN (v.)

FELICITOUS
feh LIH sih tus (adj.)

FERAL
FER ul (adj.)

FERTILE
FIR tul (adj.)

one-sidedness, partiality to one side

> After the judge's display of *favoritism* for the defendant, the plaintiff submitted a motion for a new trial.

Synonyms: preferential treatment, bias

comprehend, penetrate the meaning of

> Andrea couldn't *fathom* how a person could cheat on a test; every instinct told her it was wrong.

Synonyms: understand, grasp

suitable, appropriate; well-spoken

> The father of the bride made a *felicitous* speech at the wedding, contributing to the success of the evening.

Synonyms: proper, fitting

to pretend, give a false impression; to invent falsely

> Although Sean *feigned* indifference, he was very much interested in the contents of the envelope.

Synonyms: put on, simulate

highly productive, prolific

> Lucille had a *fertile* imagination and always conjured the most fanciful tales for her siblings.

Synonyms: abundant, fruitful

wild, brutish

> After living with gorillas for several years, Diane Fossey seemed *feral* to her more civilized contemporaries.

Synonyms: untamed, undomesticated

FORGE
FORJ (v.)

FORGERY
FORJ uh ree (n.)

FORLORN
for LORN (adj.)

FORMIDABLE
FOR mid uh bul (adj.)

FORTITUDE
FOR ti tood (n.)

FORUM
FOR um (n.)

something counterfeit or fraudulent

The *forgery* of the famous painting was close enough to the original to fool most of the experts who examined it.

Synonyms: fake, phony

to advance gradually but steadily

Despite her intense workload, Sharon *forged* ahead and graduated at the top of her class.

Synonyms: press on, progress

arousing fear or dread; inspiring awe or wonder; difficult to undertake

Realizing that she faced a *formidable* task, Barbara took a deep breath and began to clean her room for the first time in months.

Synonyms: alarming, frightening

dreary, deserted; unhappy; hopeless, depressing

Nora felt *forlorn* at the prospect of moving out of the house in which she had been born.

Synonyms: sad, dejected

public place for discussion; a public discussion

In line with its goal of finding a solution to the foreign policy issue, the university held an open *forum* to discuss suggestions by students and professors.

Synonyms: meeting, discussion

strength of mind

Although Michelle had the *fortitude* to endure a six-hour meeting, she nonetheless agreed to break it into two three-hour sessions to accommodate her less hearty coworkers.

Synonyms: strength, resilience

GLACIER
GLAY sher (n.)

GLOSSY
GLAH see (adj.)

GLUTTON
GLUT in (n.)

GOAD
GOAD (v.)

GOURMAND
goor MOND (n.)

GRACIOUS
GRAY shus (adj.)

showy, sleek

The *glossy* finish on the photographs resulted in excessive glare, making them difficult to view under direct light.

Synonyms: slick, shiny

slow-moving large mass of ice

Glaciers spanning hundreds of miles cover much of the Arctic Circle.

Synonyms: ice mass

to prod or urge

Denise *goaded* her sister Leigh into running the marathon with her because she did not want to train alone.

Synonyms: provoke, drive

person who eats and drinks excessively

Only a *glutton* could order dessert after such a rich meal.

Synonyms: gourmond, food lover

compassionate, warm-hearted

Ms. Kirchick welcomed the guests into her home and was *gracious* in offering them tea and cookies.

Synonyms: benevolent, kindly

glutton; lover of fine food

Knowing that many a *gourmand* would attend the holiday party, Melanie made sure to stock the refrigerator with extra quantities of imported cheese and gourmet sausage.

Synonyms: epicure, foodie

HACKNEYED
HAK need (adj.)

HALLMARK
HAUL mark (n.)

HARANGUE
hu RANG (n.)

HARASS
hu RASS (v.)

HAUGHTY
HAW tee (adj.)

HAZARDOUS
HAZ er duss (adj.)

specific feature, characteristc

Proper diction, a loud voice, and a compelling style are the *hallmarks* of a good public speaker.

Synonyms: trait, quality

cliched, worn out by overuse

Despite a *hackneyed* theme and a predictable storyline, the play went on to rave reviews.

Synonyms: trite, stale

irritate, torment

The mailings have become so frequent as to *harass* the recipients.

Synonyms: annoy, pester

pompous speech

Although Richard's criticism of the company threatened to derail the board meeting, the Chairman let him finish his *harangue* before adjourning.

Synonyms: tirade, rant

dangerous, risky, perilous

Though filtering has removed many *hazardous* toxins from the reservoir, the water may not yet be drinkable.

Synonyms: unsafe, harmful

condescending

The editor's *haughty* tone discouraged Nadine from submitting her short story for the literary magazine, although her writing teacher had praised it.

Synonyms: snooty, arrogant

HINDRANCE
HIN drens (n.)

HINDSIGHT
HIYND siyt (n.)

HODGEPODGE
HOJ poj (n.)

HOIST
HOYST (v.)

HUMANE
hyoo MAYN (adj.)

HYPOCRISY
hih POK rih see (n.)

perception of events after they happen

> In *hindsight,* of course, I can see that lending her the car was a big mistake because she's not a good driver.

Synonyms: retrospection

impediment, clog; stumbling block

> Not wishing to be a *hindrance* while his wife was preparing for the party, Dan and the children packed a picnic lunch and went to the park.

Synonyms: obstruction, obstacle

lift, raise

> Sam backed the pickup truck to the shed and *hoisted* the heavy crate into the back using a pulley.

Synonyms: erect, raise

jumble, mixture of assorted objects

> Instead of cooking one simple dish, Richard prepared a *hodgepodge* of different foods for the holiday meal.

Synonyms: mishmash

the profession of beliefs that one doesn't really posses

> Diane couldn't believe the *hypocrisy* of the people who claimed to believe in equal opportunities for men and women yet still refused to hire married women at their own offices.

Synonyms: insincerity, pretense

merciful, kindly

> A *humane* man, the SPCA director made sure all the animals in the shelter were well cared for.

Synonyms: caring, compassionate

IMPRESSIONABLE
im PRESH in uh bul (adj.)

IMPUGN
im PYOON (v.)

IMPUTE
im PYOOT (v.)

INACCESSIBLE
in ak SES uh bul (adj.)

INACCURATE
in AK yur it (adj.)

INARTICULATE
in ar TIK yoo lit (adj.)

to call into question, attack verbally

Even as countless allegations surfaced that *impugned* his motives, his reputation for integrity remained intact.

Synonyms: attack, hold responsible

easily influenced or affected

After attending the rock concert, the *impressionable* young girl took on the dress and mannerisms of the lead singer.

Synonyms: suggestible

unapproachable

My mother, fearing I might be *inaccessible* in the event of an emergency at home, bought me a new mobile phone.

Synonyms: unreachable, remote

to attribute; to credit

When we walked into our apartment, we *imputed* the water on the kitchen floor to leaky pipes under the sink.

Synonyms: ascribe

incomprehensible, unable to speak clearly

Carol was confident going into the debate because she knew her opponent was an *inarticulate* speaker.

Synonyms: tongue-tied, incoherent

mistaken, incorrect

Jean's guesses at Lois's age were completely *inaccurate,* so Lois finally told her the truth.

Synonyms: imprecise, wrong

INDUSTRIOUS

in DUS tree us (adj.)

INEFFABLE

in EF uh bul (adj.)

INEFFICACIOUS

in ef ih KAY shus (adj.)

INEFFICIENT

in ih FISH ent (adj.)

INEPT

in EPT (adj.)

INEVITABLE

in EV ih tu bul (adj.)

indescribable, inexpressible

Marie's first visit to the Louvre left her speechless; the *ineffable* beauty of the paintings silenced her for hours afterward.

Synonyms: beyond words, indefineable

diligent

After years of living with his *industrious* father, Ron became equally careful about his own work habits.

Synonyms: hard-working, productive

wasteful of resources, time, or energy

The chef scolded his *inefficient* staff for spending all of their time and most of their budget on the dessert course.

Synonyms: incompetent, wasteful

ineffective, incompetent

The teacher's attempts to quiet the class were *inefficacious;* she seemed invisible as the students continued to yell and leave their seats.

Synonyms: unproductive

certain

With an active effort to cut costs and raise productivity, bankruptcy is far from *inevitable* for the company.

Synonyms: inescapable, unavoidable

awkward; incapable; foolish, nonsensical

While capable of designing elegant clothing on paper, he was *inept* when it came to the real work of cutting the fabric and stitching the garments.

Synonyms: incompetent, clumsy

INHIBIT
in HIB it (v.)

INNUMERABLE
ih NOOM ur uh bul (adj.)

INORDINATE
in OR di net (adj.)

INSCRIPTION
in SKRIP shun (n.)

INSIDIOUS
in SID ee us (adj.)

INSIGHTFUL
in SIYT ful (adj.)

too many to be counted

There are *innumerable* stars in the universe.

Synonyms: countless, numerous

to hold back, prevent

John's harsh criticism *inhibited* the free exchange of ideas on the project.

Synonyms: slow down, restrain

engraving

The sword's authenticity was confirmed by the small *inscription* at the base of the blade, the signature of a well-known craftsman.

Synonyms: writing, caption

excessive, immoderate

The group was deluged by an *inordinate* number of emails complaining about their newest products.

Synonyms: unreasonable

clever, perceptive; intuitive

I never submit an article before giving it to my roommate to edit, since he always offers *insightful* comments.

Synonyms: astute, shrewd

subtly spreading harm; beguiling; alluring

Coleman's career was eventually destroyed by the *insidious* rumors that he had falsified data in his groundbreaking experiments.

Synonyms: sinister, manacing

IRONY

IY ur nee (n.)

IRRATIONAL

ih RASH ih null (adj.)

IRRESOLUTE

ih REZ uh loot (adj.)

IRREVERENT

ir REV er nt (adj.)

ISOLATED

IY suh lay tid (adj.)

JADED

JAY ded (adj.)

nonsensical, unreasonable

Rachel had an *irrational* fear of chickens, perhaps because of an unfortunate incident in her childhood on the family farm.

Synonyms: illogical, unfounded

incongruity between expectations and actualities

The *irony* of jobs becoming available in his hometown shortly after he had moved across the country in search of work was not lost on Joe.

Synonyms: paradox

disrespectful, gently or humorously mocking

Kevin's *irreverent* attitude at the History Museum was inappropriate given the serious nature of the exhibits.

Synonyms: cheeky, impertinent

undecided; indecisive, fickle

Gabriel, *irresolute* from the outset, called and cancelled at the last minute.

Synonyms: vacillating, unsure

tired by excess or overuse; slightly cynical

While the naïve girls stared at the spectacle in awe, the *jaded* matrons dozed in their chairs.

Synonyms: world-weary

solitary, singular

Though it is tempting to link the three crimes in the same neighborhood, the authorities continue to view them as *isolated* incidents.

Synonyms: exceptional, unrepeated

JEOPARDIZE
JEP er diyz (v.)

JEST
JEST (v.)

JOLLITY
JOL ih tee (n.)

JUBILATION
JOO bi LAY shin (n.)

JUSTIFY
JUS tih fiy (v.)

JUXTAPOSITION
juks ta po ZISH un (n.)

playfulness

Her comments, made in *jest,* should not be taken too seriously.

Synonyms: joke, kid

expose to injury

"Keep your voices down or you'll *jeopardize* the mission," cautioned the army captain as he led his unit on a night raid.

Synonyms: risk, endanger

joy, celebration, exultation

Tales of the team's *jubilation* became legendary when the celebration of their victory lasted an entire month.

Synonyms: elation, joyousness

cheerfulness, liveliness; celebration

Although the hostess was tense about the party, the *jollity* of her guests helped her relax.

Synonyms: gaity, jolliness

side-by-side placement

The awkward *juxtaposition* of the colorful decorations and the austere furnishings made for a confusing sight.

Synonyms: combination

to prove valid

Angered that he was being asked to *justify* his comments, the proud man stormed away without explaining what he meant.

Synonyms: validate, rationalize

KIN
KIN (n.)

LARCENY
LAR suh nee (n.)

LATENT
LAY tent (adj.)

LAVISH
LAV ish (adj.)

LEDGER
LEJ er (n.)

LEGION
LEE jun (n.)

theft of property

The crime of stealing a wallet can be categorized as petty *larceny*.

Synonyms: robbery

family, relatives

At the long awaited family reunion, *kin* gathered who had not seen each other for years.

Synonyms: relations, kith

extravagant, profuse

The *lavish* feast that followed the team's victory offered every type of food imaginable.

Synonyms: sumptuous, abundant

present but hidden; potential

When a photographic negative is exposed, the image on the film is *latent* until it is brought out with special chemicals.

Synonyms: dormant

a great number, a multitude

Legions of fans sent the movie star letters every week.

Synonyms: crowd, mass

a book that tracts finances

Amanda entered the sale into her bound *ledger* for accounting purposes and then moved on to assist the next customer.

Synonyms: accounting record

LOATH
LOHTH (adj.)

LOBBY
LOB bee (v.)

LONGEVITY
lon JEV ih tee (n.)

LUBRICATE
LOOB rih kayt (v.)

LULL
LUL (n.)

LUMMOX
LUM iks (n.)

to petition

The tobacco industry spends millions of dollars a year *lobbying* for changes in government regulations.

Synonyms: apply pressure, promote

reluctant, unwilling

Jimmy was *loath* to visit the post office because he knew he would have to wait on line for hours.

Synonyms: wary

to grease up, make slippery

In order to improve their finishing time in the Rubik's Cube competition, all the contenders *lubricate* their cubes so they will spin faster.

Synonyms: oil

long life

Legendary tales of a magical spring that ensured *longevity* inspired the voyages of countless explorers.

Synonyms: endurance

clumsy or stupid oaf

Having already broken three crystal bowls, the *lummox* was forever banned from the antiques store.

Synonyms: lout, klutz

relatively low activity

Although Sam ran into the basement when the hurricane started, he went back upstairs during a *lull* in the storm.

Synonyms: quiet period, calm

MAVERICK
MAV uh rik (n.)

MAXIM
MAK sim (n.)

MEAGER
MEE ger (adj.)

MEASURED
MEZH erd (adj.)

MECHANISM
MEHK uh nizm (n.)

MEDDLER
MED ler (n.)

fundamental principle

Abby tried her best to live her life according to the *maxim* "Do unto others as you would have them do unto you."

Synonyms: saying, adage

one who breaks away from group conformity and forges a new course

While possessing greater skill than the rest of the squad, the soldier had a reputation for being a *maverick* and therefore didn't advance in rank as quickly as the others.

Synonyms: nonconformist, individualist

calculated, deliberate

Upon coming to power, the exacting ruler took *measured* steps to improve the economy.

Synonyms: precise, considered

minimal, scanty, deficient

"How can we be expected to survive on these *meager* portions of food?" complained the hungry prisoners to the Warden.

Synonyms: insufficient, paltry

person interfering in others' affairs

Mickey is a real *meddler*, always sticking his nose where it doesn't belong.

Synonyms: busybody, pest

a machine

The *mechanism* that opens the door in a supermarket is a weight-sensor on the floor that activates a motor in the wall.

Synonyms: device, apparatus

MIFFED
MIFT (adj.)

MILESTONE
MIYL stohn (n.)

MIMIC
MIM ik (v.)

MIRAGE
mih RAZH (n.)

MISCONCEPTION
mis kon SEP shun (n.)

MISSIVE
MIS iv (n.)

important event in something or someone's history

The Nineteenth Amendment, which allowed women to vote in elections, was a *milestone* in the advancement of women's rights.

Synonyms: landmark, highlight

offended, annoyed

Roger was *miffed* at his company's refusal to employ his son even though they often hired the children of other employees.

Synonyms: peeved, chagrinned

optical illusion, apparition

After wandering the desert for hours, the group was sure they had seen a lake in the distance, but in reality it had been nothing more than a *mirage*.

Synonyms: vision, hallucination

copy, imitate

Harold worked for the circus, training monkeys to *mimic* the actions of people that walk past the cages.

Synonyms: impersonate, ape

error in understanding

It is a common *misconception* that antiques are only valuable because they are old; in reality, valuable antiques are usually examples of excellent craftsmanship from their respective eras.

Synonyms: fallacy, delusion

note or letter

Lydia spent hours composing a romantic *missive* for Leo, which she sent off in the evening mail.

Synonyms: communication

MODULATE
MOJ uh layt (v.)

MOMENTARY
MOH men TE ree (adj.)

MOMENTOUS
moh MEN tuss (adj.)

MORALITY
maw RA li tee (n.)

short-lived, lasting only for a short time

Roger's *momentary* lapse in memory suddenly ended when the officers showed him pictures of the crime scene.

Synonyms: brief, fleeting

to change pitch, intensity, or tone; to regulate

To perform the voices in her cartoon program, Jeanie *modulated* her voice to sound different for each character.

Synonyms: adjust, moderate

concerned with right and wrong

Some vegetarians aren't concerned with the *morality* of their dietary choices.

Synonyms: ethics, principles

very important or significant

Choosing to quit her job to pursue a career in acting was a *momentous* decision for Louise.

Synonyms: historic, vital

gloomy, sullen, or surly

After hearing that the university had rejected him, Lenny was *morose* for weeks.

Synonyms: miserable

marsh, an area of soggy ground

Robin stopped riding her bike through the marshland after she got stuck in the *morass* and couldn't pull her bike through.

Synonyms: mess, mire

NEGLIGIBLE
NEG lih ju bul (adj.)

NEUTRALITY
noo TRAL ih tee (n.)

NEUTRALIZE
NOO truh liyz (v.)

NITPICK
NIT pik (v.)

NONCHALANT
non shuh LAHNT (adj.)

NONDESCRIPT
non des KRIPT (adj.)

disinterest, impartiality

Switzerland is well known for its *neutrality* in times of international conflict.

Synonyms: detachment, objectivity

not worth considering

It's obvious from our *negligible* dropout rate that our students love our program.

Synonyms: insignificant, tiny

to criticize minor details

Unable to find fault with the general behavior of the company, the difficult stockholder decided instead to *nitpick* and pointed out misspellings in their correspondence.

Synonyms: carp, pick holes

to balance, offset

Dr. Schwartz poured acid in the beaker to *neutralize* the basic solution.

Synonyms: counteract, defuse

lacking interesting or distinctive qualities

The celebrity countered her glamorous image by appearing in a *nondescript* black outfit.

Synonyms: unremarkable, ordinary

calm, casual, seemingly unexcited

Humphrey Bogart was known for his *nonchalant* characters who stayed calm and composed even in the most difficult situations.

Synonyms: off hand, cool

NOSTALGIC
nah STAHL jik (adj.)

NOTABLE
NO tu bul (adj.)

NOTION
NO shin (n.)

NOVELTY
NAHV ul tee (n.)

NOVICE
NAHV is (n.)

NUDGE
NUJ (n.)

remarkable, worthy of notice

Sean didn't bother explaining the rules again because no *notable* changes had been made since the last game.

Synonyms: distinguished, prominent

longing for things of the past

After seeing her favorite movie from high school, Altoona became *nostalgic* for the clothes and games of her early teen years.

Synonyms: wistful, evocative

something new and unusual

Although sound and talking in movies is commonplace today, their introduction in the film *The Jazz Singer* was a *novelty* to audiences of the time.

Synonyms: innovation, orginial

idea or conception

Mandatory school uniforms is a *notion* that has been tossed back and forth in governments, but has never been implemented on a national scale in the United States.

Synonyms: view, concept

gentle push

In his hurry to get to the front of the line, Mark gave more than a few *nudges* to all the people around him.

Synonyms: bump, prod

beginner, apprentice

Although Jen is only a *novice* at sailing, she shows great potential and has won several races.

Synonyms: neophyte, trainee

OBSCURE
ahb SKYOOR (adj.)

OBSOLETE
ahb so LEET (adj.)

OBSTACLE
AHB stukl (n.)

OBSTINATE
AHB stu nit (adj.)

OBSTREPEROUS
ahb STREP uh res (adj.)

OBTRUSIVE
ahb TROO siv (adj.)

no longer in use; outdated

> Black-and-white television sets are now almost completely *obsolete*.

Synonyms: archaic, old-fashioned

not easily seen, inconspicuous

> Mitch loved to find *obscure* facts about random politicians to impress people with his knowledge.

Synonyms: indistinct, faint

stubborn

> The *obstinate* child could not be forced to eat any vegetables.

Synonyms: determined, inflexible

impediment

> Despite the many *obstacles* barring his way toward success, the ambitious young man was determined to succeed.

Synonyms: barrier, obstructions

pushy, too conspicuous

> I think the self-portrait that you hung in the hall is a bit *obtrusive*.

Synonyms: blatant, garish

troublesome, boisterous, unruly

> The *obstreperous* toddler, who was always breaking things, was the terror of his nursery school.

Synonyms: defiant, fractious

OPTIMISTIC
op tuh MIS tik (adj.)

OPULENCE
AHP yu lens (n.)

ORATION
aw RAY shun (n.)

ORATOR
AW ruh tur (n.)

ORDERLY
OR der lee (adj.)

ORIGINALITY
uh rij uh NAL ih tee (n.)

wealth

Livingston considered his BMW to be a symbol of both *opulence* and style.

Synonyms: luxury, affluence

expecting things to turn out well

Coach Yeats was very *optimistic* about the team's chances this year, expecting them to easily ascend to the playoffs.

Synonyms: hopeful, positive

lecturer, speaker

The new professor's dull tone of voice and lack of energy make her a particularly poor *orator*.

Synonyms: presented, narrator

lecture, formal speech

The class valedictorian gave an impressive *oration* on graduation day.

Synonyms: discourse, address

the ability to think independently

In my creative writing class, the teacher stressed the importance of *originality* in finding new topics to write about.

Synonyms: innovation, inventiveness

neat, systematic

"Please line up in an *orderly* fashion so everyone may get a ticket" the manager announced to the crowd outside the theater.

Synonyms: arranged, tidy

ORNATE
ohr NAYT (adj.)

ORTHODOX
OR thu doks (adj.)

OSTENSIBLE
ah STEN sih bul (adj.)

OSTENTATIOUS
ah sten TAY shus (adj.)

OSTRACISM
AHS tra sizm (n.)

OUTCAST
OWT kast (n.)

adhering to what is customary or traditional

> Rather than try something new and radical, the marketing analyst decided to take a more *orthodox* approach to the product and use a slogan the public was already familiar with.

Synonyms: conventional, accepted

elaborately ornamented

> The *ornate* carvings over all the doorways immediately impress visitors to the palace.

Synonyms: sumptuous, lavish

showy

> The billionaire's 200-room palace was considered by many to be an overly *ostentatious* display of wealth.

Synonyms: pretentious, flamboyant

apparent

> The *ostensible* reason for Luke's visit was to borrow a book, but secretly he wanted to chat with the lovely Wanda.

Synonyms: professed, supposed

someone rejected from a society

> The *outcast* decided that the only way to rejoin the group was to give in to their demands.

Synonyms: exile, pariah

exclusion, banishment

> Larry knew that *ostracism* would be his fate when, after he made an obnoxious comment, all the other guests at the party turned their backs to him.

Synonyms: barring, keeping out

PARADOX
PAR uh doks (n.)

PARAMOUNT
PAR uh mownt (adj.)

PARANOID
PAR uh noyd (adj.)

PARAPHRASE
PAR uh frayz (v.)

PARASITE
PAR uh siyt (n.)

PARCHED
PARCHT (adj.)

supreme, dominant, primary

It is of *paramount* importance that we make it back to camp before the storm hits.

Synonyms: chief, principle

contradiction, incongruity; dilemma, puzzle

It is a *paradox* that Susie does so well on standardized tests because her grades are not very good.

Synonyms: inconsistency, irony

to reword, usually in simpler terms

Kate adequately *paraphrased* the content of the poem, but she lost the eloquent complexity of the original.

Synonyms: summarize

exhibiting extreme mistrust of others

Leonard was very *paranoid* about losing his credit card, so he frequently checked his wallet as he walked down the street.

Synonyms: fearful, suspicious

dried up, shriveled

The *parched* hikers were relieved to finally come across a source of fresh water.

Synonyms: dry, arid

person or animal that lives at another's expense

The veterinarian checked Rover, the family dog, for all manner of common infections and *parasites*.

Synonyms: vermin

PERFIDIOUS
pir FID ee uss (adj.)

PERFUNCTORY
pir FUNK tu ree (adj.)

PERIODICALLY
pir ee ODD ikly (adv.)

PERJURE
PIR joor (v.)

PERPLEX
pir PLEKS (v.)

PERSEVERE
pir suh VEER (v.)

done in a routine manner; indifferent

> The machinelike bank teller processed the transaction and gave the waiting customer a *perfunctory* smile.

Synonyms: automatic, token

faithless, disloyal, untrustworthy

> The actress's *perfidious* companion revealed all her intimate secrets to the gossip columnists.

Synonyms: treacherous, deceitful

to tell a lie under oath

> Benson *perjured* himself to protect his son, claiming that he had spent the evening with him when in fact he had not.

Synonyms: give false testimony

from time to time; cyclically

> Although Phyllis was a devoted member of the swim team, she *periodically* allowed herself to skip practice.

Synonyms: episodically, intermittantly

to refuse to stop, regardless of difficulty

> Gail *persevered* and trekked through three feet of snow to visit her sick uncle.

Synonyms: persist, continue

to confuse

> Shawna was *perplexed* to see people shopping inside the store even though the sign said it was closed.

Synonyms: bewilder, baffle

PERSISTENCE
pir SIS tuns (n.)

PERSPICACIOUS
pur spi KAY shuss (adj.)

PERSUASIVE
pir SWAY siv (adj.)

PERTINENT
PIR tih nent (adj.)

PERVASIVE
pir VAY siv (adj.)

PESSIMISM
PES uh mizm (n.)

shrewd, astute, keen-witted

Sherlock Holmes uses his *perspicacious* mind to solve mysteries.

Synonyms: insightful, wise

the act, state, or quality of not giving up

Jamie's *persistence* at getting the petition signed amazed everyone on the team, since he was known to be quite lazy.

Synonyms: perseverance, determination

applicable, appropriate

The supervisor felt that his employee's complaints about low wages were *pertinent* and mentioned them in the salary meeting.

Synonyms: relevant, significant

convincing

Because she was such a *persuasive* negotiator, Moira's boss always sent her to meetings with difficult clients.

Synonyms: influential, credible

negativity

The player's *pessimism* was so contagious that soon the entire team believed they would lose the big game.

Synonyms: cynicism, doubt

tending to pervade, spreading throughout

Japanese animation, commonly known as anime, has proven so *pervasive* that it has even found its way into mainstream Hollywood television shows and movies.

Synonyms: encompassing, ominpresent

POMPOUS

POM pus (adj.)

POSTPONE

post POHN (v.)

POTENTATE
POH ten tayt (n.)

PRAGMATIC

prag MAT ik (adj.)

PRANK
PRANK (n.)

PREAMBLE

PRE am bul (n.)

defer, delay

> We were forced to *postpone* the championship game until after the giant snowstorm was over.

Synonyms: put off, push back

pretentious, bombastic

> We quickly turned off the television rather than listen to the *pompous* actress discuss the frivolous details of her life.

Synonyms: arrogant, self-important

practical; moved by facts rather than abstract ideals

> Susan decided to take a *pragmatic* approach to getting into college by including a number of safety schools in her applications.

Synonyms: realistic, sensible

monarch or ruler with great power

> The new *potentate* of the country instituted sweeping reforms reversing most of his predecessors policies.

Synonyms: emperor, sovereign

beginning passage

> The *preamble* to the Constitution begins with the famous phrase, "We the People of the United States…"

Synonyms: introduction, preface

practical joke

> Gary was notorious for playing tricks and *pranks* on all his coworkers.

Synonyms: trick, hoax

PRECOCIOUS
pri KOH shiss (adj.)

PREDETERMINE
pree deh TER min (v.)

PREDICTABLE
pre DIKT uh bul (adj.)

PREDOMINANT
pre DOM ih nunt (adj.)

PREPOSSESSING
pree pu ZES ing (adj.)

PRESERVE
pre ZURV (v.)

to decide in advance

Since the winners of the contest had obviously been *predetermined,* we left the raffle before the official drawing.

Synonyms: set, encode

unusually advanced or talented at an early age

The *precocious* infant had already learned a handful of words by her first birthday.

Synonyms: bright, gifted

most important or conspicuous

While many creatures inhabit J.R.R. Tolkien's Middle Earth, elves are *predominant* in the early history of the world.

Synonyms: main, principle

expected beforehand

Tired of silly, *predictable* movies, the studio decided to hire a screenwriter to devise an original story that defied all expectations.

Synonyms: unsurprising, expected

to protect, to keep unchanged

The museum keeps the ancient manuscripts locked in airtight glass containers in order to *preserve* them.

Synonyms: conserve, safeguard

attractive, engaging, appealing

The young man's *prepossessing* appearance and manner made him the most eligible bachelor at the party.

Synonyms: pleasant, alluring

PROCURE
pro KYOOR (v.)

PROD
PROD (v.)

PRODIGY
PROD ih jee (n.)

PROFANE
pro FAYN (adj.)

PROFOUND
pro FOWND (adj.)

PROFUSION
pro FYOO zhin (n.)

poke, nudge

When the dog fell asleep in the doorway, the child kept *prodding* it to wake up and move.

Synonyms: jab, push

to acquire, obtain; to get

The evidence was inadmissible in court because the police officer did not *procure* it legally.

Synonyms: secure, buy

impure; contrary to religion; sacrilegious

His *profane* comments caused him to be banished from the temple for life.

Synonyms: blasphemous, irreligious

person with exceptional talents

Her parents noticed very early that she was a math *prodigy*, capable of doing the most complex computations in her head.

Synonyms: genius, phenomenon

abundance, extravagance

There's a *profusion* of opinions on the best method for cooking duck, including roasting, frying, grilling, and many others.

Synonyms: excess, plethora

deep, meaningful; far-reaching

The audience sat silently listening to the *profound* ideas of the brilliant philosopher.

Synonyms: thoughtful, insightful

PROMULGATE
PROM ul gayt (v.)

PROPAGATE
PROP uh gayt (v.)

PROPEL
pro PEL (v.)

PROPHETIC
pro FET ik (adj.)

PROPONENT
pruh POH nent (n.)

PROPRIETY
pro PRIY ih tee (n.)

to spread out; to have offspring

The general deliberately *propagated* the rumor of a threatened invasion.

Synonyms: spread, proliferate

to make known publicly

The publicist *promulgated* the news of the celebrity's splendid wedding to the press.

Synonyms: broadcast, spread

foretelling events by divine means

The financial officer's warnings to the board of trustees proved *prophetic* as the company sank into bankruptcy.

Synonyms: visionary, predictive

to cause to move forward

"Our new ideas will *propel* this company into the next century," the executive promised.

Synonyms: drive, force

correct behavior; appropriateness

Although the princess was hungry, *propriety* demanded that she wait for the king to begin eating first.

Synonyms: decency, suitability

advocate, defender, supporter

Rose, a devoted *proponent* of animal's rights, rescued stray dogs and cats at every opportunity.

Synonyms: promoter, fan

PROSAIC
pro ZAY ik (adj.)

PROSPECT
PROSS pekt (n.)

PROSPERITY
pross PER ih tee (n.)

PROTAGONIST
pro TAG uh nist (n.)

PROTÉGÉ
PRO tuh zhay (n.)

PROTOTYPE
PRO to tiyp (n.)

possibility, a chance

The *prospect* of joining the NBA was so enticing to Stephen that he practiced basketball for ten hours every day.

Synonyms: hope, expectation

relating to prose; dull, commonplace

Simon's *prosaic* style bored his writing teacher to tears, and she dreaded having to mark his essays.

Synonyms: banal, mundane

main character in a play or story; hero

In dramatic tragedy, the *protagonist* often brings about his own downfall through a fatal character flaw.

Synonyms: central character, leading role

wealth or success

Achieving financial security and *prosperity* was a priority to Alexa, so she worked hard to get into a good college and start her path to success.

Synonyms: affluence, richness

early, typical example

When designing a computer, engineers will first build a *prototype* to test the efficiency of their design.

Synonyms: sample, model

one receiving personal direction and care from a mentor

Although David was initially a *protégé* of Pauline, he soon broke loose and developed his own style of writing.

Synonyms: star pupil

PUNDIT
PUN dit (n.)

PUNITIVE
PYOO nih tiv (adj.)

PURSUIT
pur SOOT (n.)

QUAINT
KWAYNT (adj.)

QUANDARY
KWAN du ree (n.)

QUELL
KWELL (v.)

having to do with punishment

The teacher banished Jack from the classroom as a *punitive* measure, but the boy was actually overjoyed to be missing class.

Synonyms: disciplinary, penalizing

critic; learned person

The weak politician, unable to cope with the attacks of *pundits*, resigned from office.

Synonyms: expert, authority

charmingly strange

The highlight of the street was the *quaint* little cottage that was unique amongst the high-rise apartments.

Synonyms: picturesque, odd

the act of chasing or striving

While the *pursuit* of happiness is a basic right afforded to citizens in this country, the law limits it when one person's rights interfere with the wellbeing of others.

Synonyms: hunt, search

to pacify, to suppress

While the security guards were able to *quell* the shouting inside the store, they could not do anything about the noise coming from the street.

Synonyms: subdue, control

predicament, dilemma

Laura was in a *quandary* about her plans to study abroad: What if it caused her to fall behind in her major?

Synonyms: difficulty, jam

QUERULOUS
KWER uh lus (adj.)

QUERY
KWEE ree (n.)

QUIP
KWIP (n.)

QUIZZICAL
KWIZ ih kul (adj.)

RADIANT
RAY dee unt (adj.)

RADICAL
RAD ih kul (adj.)

question

The reporters *query* about the location of the criminal's hideout annoyed the police.

Synonyms: inquiry

complaining, grumbling

His parents were tired of his *querulous* attitude and threatened to ground him if he complained anymore that night.

Synonyms: argumentative, difficult

questioning

The students stared at the teacher with *quizzical* looks as the upcoming project was outlined.

Synonyms: curious, perplexed

clever joke

Johnny Carson was an excellent talk show host because he could always come up with a funny *quip* no matter what his guests were saying.

Synonyms: witticism, wisecrack

extreme, marked departure from the norm

Bored with her appearance, Lucinda decided to make a *radical* change and dyed her hair bright purple.

Synonyms: drastic, extreme

glowing, beaming; emitting heat

Christopher looked back and smiled at his *radiant* bride as she walked down the aisle.

Synonyms: luminous, dazzling

RAZE
RAYZ (v.)

REACTIONARY
re AK shun eh ree (adj.)

REAP
REEP (v.)

REBATE
REE bayt (n.)

REBUFF
re BUFF (v.)

RECALL
re KAWL (v.)

marked by extreme conservatism, especially in politics

Despite her early years as a liberal political lobbyist, when she joined the Senate she became known as a hard-line *reactionary*.

Synonyms: backward-looking

to tear down, demolish

The house had been *razed*; where it once stood there was nothing but splinters and bricks.

Synonyms: destroy, wreck

deduction in amount to be paid

The price of the digital camera looked excessive, until I noticed that the store was offering a 50% *rebate*.

Synonyms: refund, discount

to obtain a return, often a harvest

While the grasshopper starved in the winter, the ant *reaped* the benefits of his hard labor, having so much food left over from his summer gathering.

Synonyms: gather, win

remember

Marcy's grandmother could still *recall* the hardships the family endured during the Great Depression.

Synonyms: evoke, recollect

to bluntly reject

The princess coldly *rebuffed* her suitor's marriage proposal, turning her back on him and walking away.

Synonyms: snub, slight

REINFORCE
ree in FORSS (v.)

REITERATE
re IT uh rayt (v.)

RELAPSE
ri LAPS (v.)

RELEVANCE
REL uh vens (n.)

RELINQUISH
re LIN kwish (v.)

RELISH
REH lish (v.)

to say or do again, repeat

The teacher was forced to *reiterate* her instructions because the class had not been listening the first time.

Synonyms: go over, restate

strengthen

Linda *reinforced* her argument by quoting several authoritative sources that all agree with her.

Synonyms: support, emphasize

pertinence to the matter at hand, applicability

Because the witness's testimony bore no *relevance* to the trial, the jury was instructed to disregard it.

Synonyms: significance, bearing

regress, backslide

Although he seemed to be recovering from the flu, his doctor made him stay in bed out fear that he would *relapse*.

Synonyms: revert, worsen

to enjoy greatly

Cameron *relished* the tasty sandwich, but he didn't like the bland fries that came with it.

Synonyms: savor, appreciate

to renounce or surrender something

The toddler was forced to *relinquish* the toy when the girl who owned it asked for it back.

Synonyms: give up, hand over

RELUCTANT
re LUK tant (adj.)

RELY
re LIY (v.)

REMISS
ri MISS (adj.)

REMNANT
REM nent (n.)

REMORSEFUL
re MORS ful (adj.)

REMOTE
re MOHT (adj.)

be dependant, have confidence

> The Delta Force *relied* on the intelligence supplied to them by satellite and were forced to pull back when they lost their connection.

Synonyms: depend, count

unwilling, opposing; hesitant

> Florence was *reluctant* to believe the weather report that called for snow; the news had been wrong too often in the past.

Synonyms: disinclined, averse

something left over, surviving trace

> Although most of the food was finished before he arrived at the party, Mike managed to grab some of the *remnants* before the end.

Synonyms: remains, residue

negligent about a job

> Jon was fired for being *remiss* in his duties; the company hired him to write articles, not to surf the Internet.

Synonyms: lax, careless

distant, isolated

> The island was so *remote* that Chan's cell phone wouldn't operate.

Synonyms: inaccessible, secluded

feeling sorry for wrongdoing

> After his sincere apology, Molly realized that Scott was truly *remorseful* for insulting her and decided to forgive him.

Synonyms: regretful, repentant

REPETITIVE

ruh PET uh tiv (adj.)

REPLICATE

REP lih kayt (v.)

REPRESS

re PRESS (v.)

REPRIEVE

re PREEV (n.)

REPRIMAND

REP ruh mand (v.)

REPUDIATE

re PYOO dee ayt (v.)

to duplicate, repeat

If we're going to *replicate* last year's profit margins, we're going to have to work harder.

Synonyms: copy, reproduce

done over and over again

Yasmeen disliked her job at the factory; she found doing the same task over and over to be too *repetitive* and boring.

Synonyms: recurring, cyclical

postponement of a punishment; relief from danger

The prisoner was granted a *reprieve* when the government realized he might be able to help them catch his collaborators.

Synonyms: pardon, amnesty

to restrain or hold in

Sheila *repressed* the urge to roll her eyes at the obnoxious customer.

Synonyms: contain, limit

to reject as having no authority

The old woman's claim that she was Russian royalty was *repudiated* when DNA tests showed that she was unrelated to the royal family.

Synonyms: renounce, deny

rebuke, admonish

Sarah didn't want to *reprimand* her son, but she needed to make sure he understood and obeyed her rules.

Synonyms: chastise, reproach

REPUTABLE
REH pyoo tu bul (adj.)

REQUISITION
re kwi ZIH shun (v.)

RESERVE
re ZERV (n.)

RESILIENT
re ZIL yent (adj.)

RESOLUTE
REZ uh loot (adj.)

RESOURCE
REE sors (n.)

to demand the use of

> General Montgomery *requisitioned* a new jeep to drive from his barracks to his office.

Synonyms: commandeer, appropriate

honorable, respectable

> Jeanie was excited to attend the lecture by the *reputable* scientist who is working on a cure for cancer.

Synonyms: trustworthy, honest

quick to recover, bounce back

> Luckily, Ramon was a *resilient* person and was able to pick up the pieces and move on after losing his business.

Synonyms: hardy, tough

something put aside for future use

> I couldn't borrow the textbook from the library for more than two hours because it was on *reserve* for everyone in the class to use.

Synonyms: keep, store

something that can be used

> While we'd like to be able to help our neighbors construct a new barn, we just don't have the *resources* to spare.

Synonyms: supply, source

determined; with a clear purpose

> Louise was *resolute*; she would get into medical school no matter what.

Synonyms: firm, unyeilding

RESPLENDENT
ri SPLEN dent (adj.)

RESTORE
reh STOR (v.)

RESTRAINED
ri STRAYnd (adj.)

RETAIN
ri TAYN (v.)

RETRACT
re TRAKt (v.)

REVERE
ri VEER (v.)

reestablish; revive

In an attempt to *restore* the city to its former glory, the mayor began a campaign to clean up the streets and attract businesses downtown.

Synonyms: reinstate, return

splendid, brilliant, dazzling

The bride looked *resplendent* in her long train and sparkling tiara.

Synonyms: stunning, glorious

to hold, keep possession of

Britain had to give up most of its colonies, but it *retained* control over Hong Kong until the end of the twentieth century.

Synonyms: preserve, maintain

controlled, repressed, restricted

The formerly wild girl became *restrained* and serious after a month in the strict boarding school.

Synonyms: reserved, calm

to worship, regard with awe

The whole country *revered* the President who led them out of crisis.

Synonyms: admire, respect

to take back

After Lance *retracted* his insulting remark, Vera decided to forgive him.

Synonyms: withdraw, apologize for

RHETORICAL
ri TOR ih kul (adj.)

ROSTER
ROS ter (n.)

ROUSE
ROWZ (v.)

RUDE
ROOD (adj.)

RUTHLESS
ROOTH less (adj.)

SACROSANCT
SAK roh sangkt (adj.)

a list of names

> After calling the unit to attention, Lieutenant Cole read through the *roster* to ensure that everyone was present.

Synonyms: role, register

related to using language effectively

> To prove his assertions to the crowd, the speaker asked a series of *rhetorical* questions, not actually expecting anyone to answer back.

Synonyms: metaphorical, symbolic

crude, primitive, uncouth

> Mr. Sanderson sent Geoffrey to the Principal's office because of his *rude* remarks about Roger's science project.

Synonyms: impolite, discouteous

provoke, excite, stir

> After noticing their listless play in the previous game, the cheerleaders were determined to *rouse* the basketball team to play harder in tonight's game.

Synonyms: revive, awaken

sacred

> The president regarded his early morning exercise regiment as *sacrosanct* and refused to let anything interrupt it.

Synonyms: revered, holy

merciless, compassionless

> The Terminator was a perfectly *ruthless* killer.

Synonyms: cruel, brutal

SCHOLARLY
SKOL ur lee (adj.)

SCORN
SKORN (n.)

SCOUNDREL
SKOWN drul (n.)

SCOUR
SKOWER (v.)

SCRUPULOUS
SKROOP yu luss (adj.)

SCRUTINIZE
SKROOT in iyz (v.)

contempt, derision

> The seniors felt they were superior to the rest of the school and treated the underclassmen with *scorn*.

Synonyms: disdain, disrespect

related to higher learning

> Dr. Lee studied English literature for fifteen years and published articles in a variety of *scholarly* journals.

Synonyms: learned, academic

to scrub clean

> When Kelly discovered that her in-laws were coming to visit, she *scoured* the house in an attempt to impress them.

Synonyms: polish

villain, rogue

> George the Pirate was the meanest *scoundrel* ever to roam the seas.

Synonyms: crook, rascal

to observe carefully

> When the financial managers realized the company was losing money, they hired outside consultants to *scrutinize* the billing process.

Synonyms: inspect, examine

restrained; honest; careful and precise

> David could not have stolen Carmen's money; he's too *scrupulous* to do such a thing.

Synonyms: conscientious, principled

SCURRY
SKUR ree (v.)

SECRETE
se KREET (v.)

SEDATIVE
SED uh tiv (n.)

SEQUEL
SEE kwul (n.)

SERENDIPITY
se ren DIP ih tee (n.)

SERENE
se REEN (adj.)

release fluids

The chemical *secreted* by the insect attracted its prey.

Synonyms: ooze, emit

scamper, run lightly

Robin had trouble sleeping through the noise of the squirrels that *scurried* across the roof.

Synonyms: dart, scuttle

literary or artistic work that continues a previous piece.

When the studios saw how successful the first movie was, they commissioned the director to make two *sequels*.

Synonyms: follow-up, continuation

something that calms or soothes

Marie drank warm milk, a natural *sedative*, to help her get to sleep on nights before big tests.

Synonyms: tranquilizer, relaxer

calm; peaceful

The deserted beach was *serene* and beautiful as we sat watching the sunset.

Synonyms: tranquil, still

habit of making fortunate discoveries by chance

Rosemary's *serendipity* revealed itself in many ways, such as her habit of finding money on the street.

Synonyms: destiny, luck

SHUN
SHUN (v.)

SIGNPOST
SIYN post (n.)

SKEPTICISM
SKEP tih sizm (n.)

SKIRT
SKIRT (v.)

SLUGGISH
SLUG ish (adj.)

SMUG
SMUG (adj.)

indication, guide

Although all *signposts* indicated that he was embarking on the wrong path, instinct told him to keep going.

Synonyms: marker, signal

avoid deliberately

After the unprovoked fight he started in the hall, Walter was *shunned* at school until he apologized and got help controlling his anger.

Synonyms: spurn, reject

to evade; pass close, circle around

We decided to *skirt* the city rather than risk getting caught in rush hour traffic downtown.

Synonyms: avoid, go around

disbelief; uncertainty

Despite their onlookers' *skepticism*, the Wright Brothers demonstrated that man was capable of flight.

Synonyms: doubt, cynicism

excessively self-satisfied

Roger was *smug* after he easily passed the big exam, but failing a pop quiz soon made him realize he still had to study.

Synonyms: superior, arrogant

lazy, inactive

Helga felt *sluggish* after her illness, but the doctor reassured her she would soon be back to her active self.

Synonyms: lethargic, listless

SOOTHE
SOOTHE (v.)

SOPHISTICATION
su FIS ti kay shun (n.)

SPECIOUS
SPEE shus (adj.)

SPONTANEOUS
spon TAY nee us (adj.)

SPRINT
SPRINT (v.)

SPROUT
SPROWT (v.)

worldliness, edification, enlightenment

Julia's professors noticed a new *sophistication* in her Art History papers when she returned from a semester studying in Italy.

Synonyms: urbanity, refinement

to calm, placate; comfort

Rebecca *soothed* the crying baby by rocking him and whispering comforting words.

Synonyms: pacify, quiet

on the spur of the moment, impulsive

Jean made the *spontaneous* decision to go to the movies instead of visiting her in-laws as she had planned.

Synonyms: unprompted, unplanned

plausible but incorrect

While the TV show seemed to offer sound scientific theories, educated viewers knew that most of the arguments were quite *specious*.

Synonyms: hollow, inaccurate

emerge and develop rapidly; to grow

Even though we only planted the seeds last week, the stalks have already begun to *sprout*.

Synonyms: shoot, develop

dash, run quick for short distances

When Peter realized that his package had arrived, he *sprinted* across the lawn to the front door.

Synonyms: race, hurry

SPURIOUS
SPYOOR ee uss (adj.)

SQUANDER
SKWAHN der (v.)

SQUELCH
SKWELCH (v.)

STAGNANT
STAG nent (adj.)

STATUTE
STA choot (n.)

STEALTH
STELTH (n.)

to waste

While I've been saving for a camputer, my friend Sean *squandered* all his earnings on video games.

Synonyms: spend, lavish

lacking authenticity, false

The businessman was outraged by the *spurious* accusations that he embezzled money from the company despite his spotless record.

Synonyms: bogus, fake

immobile, stale

The standing water in that *stagnant* pond is a perfect breeding ground for mosquitoes; we should drain it.

Synonyms: sluggish, inert

to suppress, to put down with force

Despite the reformer's best efforts, the company board of directors *squelched* all attempts to change office policy.

Synonyms: muffle, sensor

act of moving in a covert way

The special unit traveled by *stealth* so the enemy scouts would not detect their position.

Synonyms: furtiveness, surreptitiousness

law, edict

According to the new town *statutes*, it is illegal to throw used bubble gum onto the street.

Synonyms: decree, ruling

STUMP
STUMP (v.)

STURDY
STUR dee (adj.)

SUBMISSIVE
sub MISS iv (adj.)

SUBSIST
sub SIST (v.)

SUBSTANTIATE
sub STAN she ayt (v.)

SUBTERFUGE
SUB ter fyooj (n.)

firm, well built, stout

The contractor decided that the girders already in place were *sturdy* enough to support the rest of the house.

Synonyms: strong, powerful

to challenge; to baffle

We tried hard, but we were unable to *stump* Nate with sports trivia due to his athletic background.

Synonyms: puzzle, perplex

stay alive; survive

The young employee complained that there was no way to *subsist* on such a meager salary.

Synonyms: exist, live

tending to meekness, yielding to the will of others

The *submissive* wolf cringed at the feet of the alpha male, the leader of the pack.

Synonyms: passive, compliant

deceptive strategy

Spies who are not skilled in the art of *subterfuge* are generally exposed before too long.

Synonyms: trick, ploy

to verify, confirm, provide supporting evidence

Margo felt unwell after eating the ice cream, which *substantiated* her allergy to dairy products.

Synonyms: validate, authenticate

SUBVERT
sub VERT (v.)

SUCCUMB
su KUM (v.)

SUFFICE
suh FIYS (v.)

SULLY
SUL ee (v.)

SUMMARY
SUM uh ree (n.)

SUPERFICIAL
soo per FISH ul (adj.)

to give in to stronger power; yield

> Although the small band of warriors was clearly outnumbered, they refused to *succumb* to their enemies.

Synonyms: submit, surrender

to undermine or corrupt

> The traitor intended to *subvert* loyal citizens of the crown with the revolutionary propaganda he distributed.

Synonyms: threaten

soil, stain, tarnish, taint

> Reginald was upset to discover that the child's sticky red lollipop had *sullied* his new cashmere overcoat.

Synonyms: smear, denegrate

meet requirements, be capable

> Although I would have liked to meet with the Vice President of productions, the Vice President of marketing will *suffice*.

Synonyms: be sufficient, be adequate

hasty; shallow and phony

> The politician was friendly, but his *superficial*, fixed smile indicated he might not be sincere.

Synonyms: surface, external

shortened version; abstract

> The movie's plot proved to be so complicated that the director had one of the characters give a *summary* of events to explain the story.

Synonyms: synopsis, outline

SURREPTITIOUS
sir up TISH iss (adj.)

SURROGATE
SUR uh git (n.)

SUSPEND
su SPEND (v.)

SWARM
SWARM (n.)

SWERVE
SWERV (v.)

SYCOPHANT
SIK u fant (n.)

a substitute; one filling in for someone else

> Cheryl's best friend Lisa was more like a *surrogate* sister, since Cheryl's own sister was ten years older than her.

Synonyms: replacement, stand-in

secret, stealthy

> The dissenting members of the committee scheduled a *surreptitious* meeting among themselves to discuss how best to advance their unpopular agenda.

Synonyms: sneaky, sly

a large number of insects traveling in a group

> When we saw the *swarm* of bees flying toward the lemonade stand, we shouted for everyone to run away.

Synonyms: throng, pack

to defer, interrupt; dangle, hang

> Construction of the building was *suspended* when the contractor ran out of bricks.

Synonyms: postpone, delay

self-serving flatterer; yes-man

> It appears that the executive would rather have a *sycophant* than a truly capable assistant who might occasionally disagree with him.

Synonyms: toady

to turn from a straight course

> When the driver saw the pickup truck coming straight at him, he slammed on his breaks and *swerved* off of the road.

Synonyms: veer, turn sharply

SYMMETRY
SIM eh tree (n.)

SYNERGY
SIN er jee (n.)

SYNTHESIZE
SIN thi siyz (v.)

TACT
TAKT (n.)

TALISMAN
TAL iss man (n.)

TANGENTIAL
tan JEN shul (adj.)

combined action producing greater results

Improved *synergy* among the team members helped to produce a better product than the same team had developed a year earlier.

Synonyms: cooperation, conjunction

equality and balance in objects

Gladys's teachers were very impressed with the *symmetry* of her paintings; they thought she showed remarkable attention to detail for a first-grader.

Synonyms: regularity, evenness

consideration in dealing with others, skill in not offending others

We asked Keisha to talk to the teacher about extending our deadlines because, as the most polite one amongst us, she would ask with the most *tact*.

Synonyms: diplomacy, discretion

to produce artificially; to create through combination of different elements

Because the guitar sounded so real, we were surprised to learn that the music had been *synthesized* in a computer.

Synonyms: create, make

digressing, diverting

Your argument is interesting, but it is *tangential* to the matter at hand, so I suggest we get back to the point.

Synonyms: peripheral, divergent

magic object that offers supernatural protection

The shop was selling *talismans* that were rumored to protect the owner from car accidents.

Synonyms: amulet, charm

TANGIBLE
TAN ji bul (adj.)

TAUNT
TAWNT (v.)

TEMERITY
te MEH ri tee (n.)

TEMPERANCE
TEM per unss (n.)

TENACIOUS
ten AY shiss (adj.)

TENTATIVE
TEN tu tiv (adj.)

to ridicule, to mock, insult

Gary sat in a corner of the playground crying because the other children had *taunted* him for wearing a shirt they deemed unfashionable.

Synonyms: tease, sneer at

able to be sensed, perceptible, measurable

The storming of the castle didn't bring the soldiers *tangible* rewards, but it brought them great honor.

Synonyms: touchable, real

self-control, moderation

As a reward for the *temperance* he had demonstrated all week, the athlete indulged in his favorite soft drink and a slice of pizza.

Synonyms: constraint, restraint

recklessness, fearlessness

We couldn't believe her *temerity* as she climbed up the side and looked over the edge of the Hoover Dam.

Synonyms: nerve, audacity

not fully worked out; uncertain

Even after meeting for hours, the committee was only able to agree on a *tentative* plan because of the strong conflicting opinions of its members.

Synonyms: hesitant, cautious

determined, keeping a firm grip on

The gymnast was *tenacious* in clinging to the parallel bars after he lost his grip in the middle of an earlier routine.

Synonyms: stubborn, resolute

TESTIMONY
TESS ti moh nee (n.)

THERAPEUTIC
ther uh PYOO tik (adj.)

THICKET
THIK et (n.)

THRONG
THRONG (n.)

THWART
THWART (v.)

TIMELESS
TIYM les (adj.)

medicinal

Trent found the hot springs to be very *therapeutic* for his aches and pains, so he bathed in them often.

Synonyms: healing, curative

statement made under oath

The eyewitness *testimony* proved decisive as the jury deliberated the verdict.

Synonyms: proof, evidence

a large group of people, crowd

Glenda squeezed through the *throngs* of people who had gathered to see the fireworks on Independence Day.

Synonyms: multitude, mass

dense bushes

Larry tried catching his neighbor's kitten when it got loose, but it ran into the *thicket* behind the house and was soon completely hidden.

Synonyms: undergrowth, brush

eternal, ageless

Although ideals of beauty change over the years, Marilyn Monroe's appeal has proven *timeless*.

Synonyms: enduring, everlasting

to block or prevent from happening; frustrate

Thwarted in his attempt to get at the food secured inside the cooler, the bear stomped away from the campground.

Synonyms: prevent, foil

TIMOROUS
TIM uh rus (adj.)

TOADY
TOH dee (n.)

TOLERATE
TOL uh rayt (v.)

TONIC
TON ik (n.)

TORPID
TOR pid (adj.)

TOUCHSTONE
TUCH stohn (n.)

flatterer, hanger on, yes-man

> The king was surrounded by *toadies* who rushed to agree with whatever outrageous comment he made.

Synonyms: sycophant, creep

timid, shy, full of apprehension

> Lois, a *timorous* woman, relied on her children to act for her whenever aggressive behavior was called for.

Synonyms: nervous, fearful

a promoter of physical or mental health

> Lukewarm grapefruit juice was my least favorite of the various *tonics* prescribed by my grandmother.

Synonyms: remedy, cure

to endure, permit; to respect others

> Pedro was unable to *tolerate* the noise from below any longer, so he went downstairs to ask his neighbor not to play the drums at four in the morning.

Synonyms: stand, bear

something used to test the excellence of others, standard

> Style and sensibility are the *touchstones* of a successful movie director.

Synonyms: criterion, benchmark

lethargic; unable to move; dormant

> The *torpid* surgery patient waited patiently for the anesthesia to wear off.

Synonyms: lazy, stagnant

TOURNIQUET
TOOR ni kit (n.)

TRACTABLE
TRAK te bul (adj.)

TRAIT
TRAYT (n.)

TRANQUIL
TRAN kwil (adj.)

TRANSCRIBE
tran SKRIYB (v.)

TRANSIENT
TRANZ ee ent (adj.)

easily managed or controlled

Lucy was always a very *tractable* child; it was only in her teenage years that she began to rebel.

Synonyms: obedient, dutiful

bandage that pressures an artery in order to stop bleeding

Though advocated in days of old, administering a *tourniquet* to victims of severe cuts is now frowned upon by the medical establishment.

Synonyms: bandage, tight wrap

peaceful, calm, composed

The ship's captain looked over at the *tranquil* sea, which was motionless and glassy.

Synonyms: serene, still

distinguishing feature; quality

While Mary Ann and Georgie share many *traits*, their identical sense of humor stands out the most.

Synonyms: attribute, characteristic

temporary, short-lived, fleeting

The actor's moment in the spotlight proved to be *transient* when her play closed due to poor reviews.

Synonyms: brief, passing

reproduce, record

After the meeting, a secretary *transcribed* the entire conversation from a tape recording she had made.

Synonyms: write out, copy

TRANSPARENT
trans PAR ent (adj.)

TRAVESTY
TRA ves tee (n.)

TREACHERY
TRECH uh ree (n.)

TREATISE
TREE tiss (n.)

TREMULOUS
TREM yoo luss (adj.)

TRIGGER
TRIG er (v.)

parody, exaggerated imitation, caricature

> When the jaywalker was sentenced to life in prison, many observers called it a *travesty* of justice because of the relative triviality of his crime.

Synonyms: charade, mockery

see-through, invisible

> When the glass door is cleaned, it becomes virtually *transparent*.

Synonyms: clear, translucent

formal discourse on a subject

> The *treatise* on Hawthorne that Mary presented at the conference went on to become a chapter in her book on the subject.

Synonyms: dissertation, essay

willful betrayal of trust

> When the president's closest advisor turned against him in the revolution, it was the ultimate act of *treachery*.

Synonyms: deceit, treason

to set off, initiate

> One carelessly discarded cigarette butt was enough to *trigger* a forest fire due to exceptionally dry conditions.

Synonyms: activate, generate

trembling; quivering; fearful, timid

> The *tremulous* stray cat approached cautiously as the boy offered a bowl of milk.

Synonyms: unsteady, shaky

UNDERMINE
un der MIYN (v.)

UNETHICAL
un ETH ih kul (adj.)

UNFETTER
un FET er (v.)

UNHERALDED
un HER ul did (adj.)

UNIQUE
yoo NEEK (adj.)

UNIVERSAL
yoo ni VER sal (adj.)

not conforming to approved behavior; immoral

Roger was summoned to a disciplinary meeting to discuss his multiple instances of *unethical* behavior this past week.

Synonyms: unprincipled, wrong

to sabotage, thwart

Rumors of his infidelities *undermined* the star's marriage, which soon ended in divorce.

Synonyms: weaken, undercut

unexpected, not publicized

The gallant knight's arrival was *unheralded*, so the princess was surprised to discover him in the castle.

Synonyms: not known, unannounced

to free from restrictions

After finding the broken leash, the dog owner wondered where his pet would go now that it was *unfettered*.

Synonyms: release, liberate

worldwide; applicable to anything

Because of her *universal* appeal, the internationally acclaimed actress was the perfect spokeswoman for the charity auction.

Synonyms: widespread, general

one of a kind, unequaled

Every snowflake is *unique*; no two are exactly alike.

Synonyms: sole, single

USURP
yoo SURP (v.)

UTILITARIAN
yoo til ih TAYR ee un (adj.)

UTOPIA
yoo TOH pee uh (n.)

VACANT
VAY kent (adj.)

VACILLATE
VAS uh layt (v.)

VAGUE
VAYG (adj.)

efficient, functional, useful

I have no doubt that these *utilitarian* solutions to the budget problems will be well received.

Synonyms: practical, effective

to take over without right

The minister *usurped* the throne from the current king and had him imprisoned.

Synonyms: appropriate, seize

empty, unoccupied

A squirrel took up residence in the *vacant* birdhouse.

Synonyms: unfilled, free

perfect place

Wilson's idea of *utopia* was a beautiful, sunny beach on a tropical island.

Synonyms: Eden, paradise

inexplicit, ambiguous, indistinct

We had to go back to the professor for clearer directions because the ones posted at the class website were too *vague* to follow.

Synonyms: unclear, hazy

to waver, show indecision

The customer held up the line as he *vacillated* between ordering chocolate or coffee ice cream.

Synonyms: hesitate, dither

VARIED
VAR eed (adj.)

VARIEGATED
VAR ee uh gay tid (adj.)

VAST
VAST (adj.)

VEER
VEER (v.)

VENERABLE
VEN er a bul (adj.)

VENERATE
VEN uh rayt (v.)

varied; marked with different colors

The *variegated* foliage of the jungle enables thousands of different animal species to hide there.

Synonyms: multicolored, dappled

diverse; modified

We usually get a *varied* crowd at our weekly meetings.

Synonyms: mixed, various

alter direction, turn

"After the next traffic light, make a left and then *veer* right at the fork," I instructed the cabdriver as he drove me home.

Synonyms: swerve, bend

immense, enormous, great in size or intensity

Because of her *vast* knowledge of random trivia, Margaret was an expert game show contestant.

Synonyms: huge, gigantic

respect, admire, revere

Her classmates *venerated* Shakira after she won the statewide writing contest three years in a row.

Synonyms: worship, idolize

respected because of age

All the villagers sought the *venerable* old woman's advice whenever they had a problem.

Synonyms: esteemed, revered

VENGEANCE
VEN jinss (n.)

VERDANT
VUR dnt (adj.)

VERIFY
VER ih fiy (v.)

VERISIMILITUDE
ver uh SIH mil ih tood (n.)

VESTIGE
VES tij (n.)

VEX
VEKS (v.)

green with vegetation

He wandered deeply into the *verdant* woods in search of mushrooms and other edible flora.

Synonyms: lush, fertile

retribution

While their actions against the homeowner were wrong, his act of *vengeance* was far worse.

Synonyms: revenge, reprisal

quality of appearing true or real

The TV show's *verisimilitude* led viewers to believe that the characters it portrayed were real.

Synonyms: semblance of truth

substantiate, confirm

Before we can go any further with the experiment, we need to *verify* that the results we've obtained are accurate.

Synonyms: prove, validate

to irritate, annoy, confuse, puzzle

The old man, who loved his peace and quiet, was *vexed* by his neighbor's loud music.

Synonyms: displease, irk

trace, remnant

Vestiges of the former tenant still remained in the apartment, even though he hadn't lived there for years.

Synonyms: sign, hint

VICARIOUS
viy KAYR ee us (adj.)

VIGILANT
VIJ uh lent (adj.)

VIGNETTE
vin YET (n.)

VIGOROUS
VIG uh rus (adj.)

VILE
VIYL (adj.)

VILLAINOUS
VIL uh nus (adj.)

attentive, watchful

Our community members must remain *vigilant* if we are to discover the identities of the vandals.

Synonyms: alert, wary

secondhand experience, endured on behalf of another

Although Yuri had never traveled outside his hometown, he felt the *vicarious* thrill of adventure through the novels he read daily.

Synonyms: surrogate, indirect

energetic, robust; healthy; active

Following a *vigorous* workout at the gym, Shelley liked to treat herself to a cold iced tea.

Synonyms: dynamic, vital

decorative design; short literary composition

The writer's clever little *vignette* was published in a respected literary magazine.

Synonyms: sketch

offensive, obnoxious, wicked

When the public learned of the Duke's *villainous* plot to overthrow the king, they stormed his home and dragged him straight to the royal palace.

Synonyms: infamous, bad

loathsome, disgusting, offensive, wretched

When we worked in the chemistry lab, we needed to mix many of the chemicals in a special airshaft that protected us from the *vile* odors they produced.

Synonyms: evil, despicable

VINDICTIVE

vin DIK tiv (adj.)

VIRTUOSO

VUR choo oh so (n.)

VIRULENT

VIR yu lint (adj.)

VISCOUS

VIS kus (adj.)

VITAL

VIY tul (adj.)

VITIATED

VISH ee ay tid (adj.)

someone with masterly skill; expert musician

The conductor is a *virtuoso* and has performed in all the most prestigious concert halls.

Synonyms: skilled, expert

spiteful, vengeful, unforgiving

The *vindictive* loser tripped the winner of the spelling bee the next day at school.

Synonyms: malicious, bitter

thick, syrupy, and sticky

The *viscous* sap trickled slowly down the trunk of the tree.

Synonyms: glutinous, gummy

extremely infectious; irritating, harsh or hateful

Alarmed at the *virulent* hate mail, the movie star decided to hire a bodyguard.

Synonyms: bitter, spiteful

impaired; corrupted

The soup became bland and *vitiated* after too much water had been added.

Synonyms: weaken, blight

urgently necessary, critical

The nurse sat with the patient checking her heart rate and blood pressure until all of her *vital* signs were back to normal.

Synonyms: essential, crucial

VIVID
VIV id (adj.)

VULGAR
VUL ger (adj.)

WANE
WAYN (v.)

WARY
WAYR ee (adj.)

WATERSHED
WOT er shed (n.)

WAVER
WAY ver (v.)

crudely indecent; boorish; ostentatious

> Samantha refused to eat a meal with Howard again; she found his *vulgar* jokes to be offensive.

Synonyms: rude, offensive

bright and intense in color; strongly perceived

> The *vivid* colors of the rose garden were visible from miles away.

Synonyms: vibrant, brilliant

careful, cautious

> The dog was *wary* of Bola at first, only gradually letting its guard down and wagging its tail when he came home at night.

Synonyms: discreet, suspicious

decline, decrease in size or intensity

> The new shortstop saw his popularity begin to *wane* immediately after the serious error.

Synonyms: diminish

move unsteadily back and forth; hesitate, falter

> Because her husband continued to *waver*, Mildred decided to order dinner for him.

Synonyms: dither, vacillate

critical turning point

> The invention of sound in film was a *watershed* in the development of modern cinema.

Synonyms: dividing moment

WHEEDLE
WEED l (v.)

WHITTLE
WIT l (v.)

WILY
WHY lee (adj.)

WRATH
RATH (n.)

YIELD
YEELD (v.)

ZEPHYR
ZEH fuhr (n.)

shape wood with a knife

The skillful craftsman *whittled* a crest onto the old oak door.

Synonyms: carve, cut

to obtain through flattery

Frank *wheedled* the other students into doing his work for him.

Synonyms: coax, cajole

forceful anger

Hillary feared her father's *wrath* when she told him that she wrecked his car.

Synonyms: rage, fury

clever, deceptive

Yet again, the *wily* coyote managed to elude the ranchers who wanted to capture it.

Synonyms: crafty, cunning

A gentle breeze; something airy or insubstantial

The *zephyr* from the ocean made the intense heat on the beach bearable for the sunbathers.

Synonyms: breath, draft

surrender, concede; be productive

When we have a disagreement about sports trivia, I *yield* to Brian because of his overwhelming knowledge of the subject.

Synonyms: defer, capitulate